Yes, Ma'am

Yes, Ma'am

The Secret Life of Royal Servants

Tom Quinn

Biteback Publishing

First published in Great Britain in 2025 by
Biteback Publishing Ltd, London
Copyright © Tom Quinn 2025

ISBN 978-1-78590-846-0

10 9 8 7 6 5 4 3 2 1

A CIP catalogue record for this book is available from the British Library.

Set in Adobe Caslon Pro

Printed and bound in Great Britain by
CPI Group (UK) Ltd, Croydon CR0 4YY

FSC
www.fsc.org
MIX
Paper | Supporting
responsible forestry
FSC® C013604

Contents

'One doesn't think much about one's ancestors…
They might be a rather bad influence.'
– Queen Elizabeth II, to the author

'There is, at all Courts, a chain, which connects the Prince, or the
Minister, with the Page of the Back-stairs, or the Chambermaid.
The King's Wife, or Mistress, has an influence over him; a Lover
has an influence over her; the Chambermaid, or the Valet de
Chambre, has an influence over both; and so ad infinitum.'
– Lord Chesterfield, *Letters on the Art of Becoming
a Man of the World and a Gentleman, 1774*

Introduction

*'Children? Yes, I suppose some people
see them as a sort of punishment...'*
– Prince Philip, to the author

We are all intrigued by our own family histories and when we begin to delve into the past, most of us discover that long ago – and sometimes not so long ago – a family member worked as a servant. This is hardly surprising given that in 1900 there were an astonishing one and a half million people in the United Kingdom working as domestic servants.

Most were women from poorer backgrounds who were expected to work twelve-hour days six or six and a half days a week from the age of twelve or fourteen.

My own interest in the lives of domestic servants – including royal servants – began with my mother's stories of working as a fifteen-year-old kitchen maid in a big house in Ireland in the 1940s. Much of the work was back-breaking and tedious, but the saving grace was, as my mother put it, 'those marvellous girls I worked with; the great gossip we had and the fun'. The fun included swimming in a lake on the estate, sleeping on the roof on hot nights in summer, shinning up a tree to escape the attentions of a 'frisky gardener' and gossiping about the family. For servants of the British royal family, the work might be just as exhausting, but there could be even more fun – who, after all, could resist life in a great palace, where so often even a humble kitchen maid became privy to the secrets of one of the most famous families in the world?

For centuries, servants were cheap and so the houses of the rich expanded, as it were, to accommodate them. Indeed, by the end of the nineteenth century, country houses were being built on such a scale that the servants often had to run from the kitchen to the dining room if the food was to be served warm.

After the introduction of inheritance tax and the changes wrought by two world wars, the vast houses and their rolling parkland found themselves deserted by servants, who preferred factory work. The mansions became unmanageable or were simply abandoned, and they began to be demolished: more than 1,000 big country houses were torn down in the century after 1875, according to the curators of a famous 1974 exhibition at London's Victoria and Albert Museum.

But while all this was going on, one family at least was able to keep its mansions and palaces going, continuing to employ vast numbers of servants, as it still does today: the royal family.

For this glimpse into the hidden world of the royal servant I have themed each chapter to see how, for example, the kitchen staff or the ladies in waiting have changed over the centuries. To this I have added stories told to me by royal staff on the strict understanding that informants' identities were protected. Some royal staff jobs have now vanished, but even when those jobs were filled there was something mysterious and highly secretive about them – what exactly did royal jesters and fools do, for example, and why were they employed for so long? There are also chapters on the outdoor staff – the gillies and gamekeepers – as well as chapters on what goes on in royal bedrooms and in the kitchens.

In this book I've tried to avoid over-emphasising the dull routine of a royal servant's life; there is little need for a blow-by-blow account of the servant's day, nor for a precise account of who reported to whom and exactly what each was paid. Instead, I have tried to provide a more impressionistic account of the world of royal service, an account that focuses more on the telling anecdote than on the exact tally of buckets of coal carried upstairs at Buckingham Palace or Balmoral. I've included servant tales that bring to life the ups and downs, the eccentricities and intimacies of such close proximity to the only family in Britain that still lives, in the domestic sphere at least, as it did in the eighteenth century.

The idea is to get behind the surface view of royal service, a view with which we are already familiar and which can be read about in countless books. In order to find out what really goes on below stairs – and indeed on the backstairs – we need to go through the green baize door to the hidden world that supports a small number of glittering stars – the kings and queens, princes and princesses we know almost too well.

Here you will find the stories of the equerry who threatened to throw Queen Victoria out of her own stables, the king who preferred his parrot to his children, the courtiers who couldn't understand a word their new king said.

Other stories include the tale of the junior footman who had to change his name because Queen Victoria was horrified to learn he was called Albert (how dare a servant have the same name as her beloved husband!); how the late Queen Mother fell into the arms of one of her gillies while fishing and would regularly shout at the salmon in the river Dee at Balmoral; and how Prince Edward once told his driver to stop looking in his rear-view mirror.

Moving closer to the present, we find Queen Elizabeth II trying to fix a picnic table and insisting that using a screwdriver is far more difficult than being queen; Prince Philip worrying that if his son Charles read too much poetry, it might make him gay; and Prince Philip's mother regularly setting fire to her rooms at Buckingham Palace.

The final part of the book looks at the huge complexities of living with royal staff in the modern world; seeing life through the eyes of staff at Kensington Palace, for example, we glimpse Meghan Markle dancing with Prince William and terrifying an Old Etonian equerry by trying to hug him!

Perhaps most intriguing of all, we see, through the shrewd commentary of serving and retired staff, how the relationship between Meghan and Harry and William and Kate started with high hopes, fun and happiness and slowly descended into bitterness and anger.

As this book tries to show, the lives of royal servants, from below-stairs staff to senior advisers, give us a unique and uniquely intriguing glimpse into the royal family, ancient and modern. Here you can see them – everyone from the grandest courtier to the humblest kitchen maid – as they have never been seen before.

Chapter One

Why everyone wants a servant

*'I never liked animals quite as much as my wife or children
 – except eating them of course.'*
– PRINCE PHILIP

To understand the secret lives of royal servants, it is essential to understand the history of monarchy and the social hierarchies that underpin it, because those hierarchies have survived remarkably unchanged from medieval times right up to the present.

In the Middle Ages, everyone, from earl to kitchen maid, was effectively the servant of the monarch. Kings controlled the lives and fortunes of the landed aristocracy; the aristocracy controlled everyone else. The vast bulk of the population could be described as landless, illiterate serfs. They had no rights and no property; their daughters and wives and they themselves were entirely at the disposal of the local landed aristocrat. That aristocrat in turn held his land entirely at the whim of the monarch. All the most senior aristocrats in the land – the barons, earls, lords, knights and baronets – worked with and for the monarch because to do otherwise was to arouse suspicion. A great lord who did not attend court would quickly fall under suspicion: he must be plotting rebellion. Why else would he not attend his king, his lord?

So, in a sense, in this early period everyone was a servant and every class, except the very lowest, in turn had their own servants. Servants, as serfs or villeins, were effectively property in the Middle Ages and then slowly over the centuries they became paid servants and then, as they are known today, staff. To own villeins, to have servants and to pay domestic staff was and remains a key part of what makes the aristocracy and the royal family different from the rest of us.

The highest ambition of the aristocracy and the royal family traditionally is to show that they do nothing menial for themselves. When the rising middle classes grew wealthier in England in the eighteenth century, they wanted above all else to ape royalty and the aristocracy by also paying others to do their dirty work. To be part of the leisured classes was to have arrived. And this aspiration lasted well into the twentieth century and to some extent continues into the twenty-first.

I can remember my own mother-in-law's proudest boast was that she had never had to work; she had employed a full-time nurse for her children as well as a nanny, a cleaner, a gardener and a housekeeper. She always looked astonished when I asked what she did while the nurses and nannies were looking after the children. 'Why, nothing I suppose, but I had a busy social life having tea with friends and shopping.'

This desire of the middle classes – even the lower-middle

classes – to have at least one servant – a maid of all work, as she was known in the nineteenth and early twentieth centuries – was linked to the desire to move up the social scale. Only the very poorest could not afford at least one skivvy. Aristocrats might have hundreds of servants. The monarch might have as many as a thousand.

Servants conferred status; the British obsession with class held and still holds that the highest social classes are most esteemed because they can afford to pay other people to do everything for them.

This book is about royal servants and their relationships with each other and with those who employed them, but it is also about how royal servants themselves sought status by having servants of their own; the world below stairs was just as socially stratified as the upstairs world of kings and queens. Well into the twentieth century, senior servants treated lowlier servants with the same kind of disdain and haughtiness with which they themselves were treated by those who employed them and by those who were even farther up the servant hierarchy.

Of course, the higher up the social scale one happened to be, the greater the range of servants, until at the very top we find the royal family keeping people to work for them but also, in earlier times, to amuse them; at its worst, the royal family even kept people as little more than pets. These, if you like, are the secret servants of the royal family whose lives we will try to explore in this book.

Then there are the vast numbers of servants who were em-ployed rather than simply kept – though, as we will see, the line between being kept as a companion and employed as a member of staff was often blurred. Henry VIII kept a fool, a jester, who was fed and clothed but never paid. Elizabeth II paid her senior staff, her courtiers, but many of them felt – as they would have felt with no other employer – that they simply could not leave and seek employment elsewhere and were lucky to be offered the chance to be royal companions, paid or unpaid. As they had numerous servants themselves, being a royal companion gave them something to do that was not tainted by the idea it might involve any work.

Queen Victoria's ladies in waiting were paid handsomely, but they would have been horrified at the suggestion that they were really just foot soldiers in that army of people paid to be at the beck and call of the monarch. It was only snobbery and an obsession with status that refused to accept that a paid companion wasn't that different from a paid nanny or footman or gardener.

* * *

The secret lives of all royal servants, whether companions or below-stairs staff, are fascinating, and though we can only piece together their lives in earlier ages through historical records, many of which have only become available more recently, the situation is easier as we move into the late nineteenth and twentieth centuries.

Many of the dozens of royal staff I have spoken to over the past four decades can recall life as a servant in the royal palaces going back to the 1890s because their parents and sometimes grandparents were also employed by the royal family.

One of the interesting changes this book also examines is how 'servant' became a dirty word; all royal servants are now known as royal staff. The change is a recognition that historically there was always something slightly demeaning about being a servant – what Victorian domestic servants called the 'shame of cap and apron'.

What made being a servant demeaning was not the work itself but the acknowledgement by society itself that servants were a lower sort; they were inherently inferior to their masters, whether royal or otherwise.

And it is certainly true that we have moved from employers, including royal employers, deliberately emphasising their superiority to a situation where, quite rightly, royal employers are permanently terrified they will be accused of treating their servants as inferiors.

But what was formerly explicit is now implicit. The royal family now treat their staff with consideration and at least superficially as equals, but the old social barriers are still there and just as difficult to cross as ever they were.

Where medieval servants often slept on the floor, a member of the royal staff today may have his or her own flat at Buckingham Palace or a cottage in the grounds of Windsor Castle. But he or she will not be invited to tea.

There has been a vast change in attitudes, but deference, however uneasily maintained, is always there. Even today we suffer from a lingering sense of awe at the idea of the landowning aristocracy, which is to a large extent what royalty is; we think of them as somehow special. To work for them in any capacity is, for some, to be especially privileged; to work for the royal family, the ultimate aristocratic family, even more so.

Royal staff frequently stay in post for life and they are fiercely protective of their royal employers' secrets. It is almost as if some version of the famous Stockholm syndrome is at work: we may recall that kidnap victims often grow to sympathise with, even, support their captors. Something similar happens with royal staff and it is a phenomenon as old and as inexplicable as the royal family itself.

*   *   *

There has always been something secretive about life in royal service – the royal family don't really want people to know exactly what the royal gamekeepers do to ensure there are enough pheasants for a shooting day, for example. They don't, as Princess Margaret famously said, want to tell people what they had for breakfast or what sort of loo paper they use. They don't want the private thoughts of below-stairs staff to be more widely known, but the royal family – or The Firm as the late Diana Spencer called it, using a phrase coined by her father-in-law, Prince Philip – employs a wide range of people from an extraordinary range of backgrounds and as with any group of disparate people who work together there are disagreements, petty jealousies and examples of outrageous and eccentric behaviour. Life as a servant in the royal family is by turns bizarre, entertaining, mundane, intriguing and rich in gossip and backbiting.

Perhaps most interesting of all are the stories the servants have to tell about their day-to-day experiences living with and attending to members of the royal family. Some of these stories reflect badly on individual royals, but others show the kindness and deep affinity royal family members occasionally have with their staff – and, as we will see, both aspects of servant life in the royal family have been true for as long as we have had a royal family.

The curious nature of royal service – that staff often feel uniquely privileged, just as their ancestor servants must have felt – has two important effects: first it tends to engender loyalty, especially if the staff are aristocratic companions (courtiers and ladies in waiting), and it occasionally creates uniquely close bonds even between relatively lowly staff and their masters. It is this close bond, an intimacy that does not always happen in other areas of employment, that has produced many of the stories recounted here. They are stories that reveal the strange, amusing, often bizarre, but until now largely concealed side of a unique family and a unique way of life.

Many biographers and historians today adopt a chiding tone – we writers are constantly on the lookout for ways in which the past fails to live up to our standards. It is as if we cannot believe that our own mores will, in turn, come to seem foolish, archaic, perhaps callous, a century or more from now; I have kept that very much in mind while writing this book.

Much of *Yes, Ma'am* concerns how history, and especially the history of the royal family, is about making friends and influencing people. We like to think that nepotism, jobs for the boys – whatever we like to call it – is largely a thing of the past or a thing that afflicts dictatorships elsewhere in the world but not us. In fact, nothing could be further from the truth.

Britain never scores particularly well on the Transparency International corruption perceptions index because corruption is embedded in today's society much as it was in the past. Let's take a few examples: a large payment to a political party will often guarantee a peerage; ministers and MPs regularly leave political life and move into extremely lucrative jobs with private companies who are employing them solely in the hope that they will be able to influence former colleagues in Parliament; some ministers leave politics and within months have secured a dozen or more lucrative jobs for which they have few qualifications other than their previous influential positions. One former Cabinet minister left politics to become the editor of a national newspaper while having little experience as a journalist.

So, when we look at the past, at the royal court in Tudor, Elizabethan or Victorian times, we should resist the temptation to condemn. As power shifted from the royal family to Parliament, corruption moved with it, but the royal family's social status remained and for those who love status, the appeal of working as a servant for the royal family remains as strong as ever.

* * *

In the next chapter, I look back at the history and context of power that has produced the modern royal servant. That he or she feels different from other servants, and indeed from people doing other paid jobs, is entirely the product of more than a thousand years of royal and aristocratic history.

Chapter Two

Everyone is owned by the king

---

*'We have school fees and staff to pay, houses to keep up
– that's why we get paid rather a lot.'*
– Former courtier, author interview

'I hope I'm not a tourist attraction.'
– William, Prince of Wales

After William the Conqueror's victory at Hastings in 1066, everything in England became – overnight, as it were – the new king's property. And by everything we really do mean everything – land, houses, animals and people, with the possible exception of the many religious houses, monasteries and abbeys. These last were nominally the new king's property, but no English king at this time would have interfered with a realm under the jurisdiction of the Pope.

Land owned by William by right of conquest is still owned by the crown. Even today, the presumption is that if land can't be proved to belong to someone else, it is the crown's. And what does the crown own? Well, it owns 286,000 acres of agricultural land in the UK; it owns all of London's Regent Street and half of St James's; it owns more than half the UK's foreshore (coastal land under water at high tide) and it owns all the gas, oil and coal under the seabed out to twelve miles from the coast.

Crown Estate profits in 2023/24 reached £1.04 billion. Now, only a portion of this goes to the royal family, but the amount is decided not by Parliament but privately by the Prime Minister in private consultation with the royal household. The monarchy gets 12 per cent of Crown Estate profits each year (known as the sovereign grant) and the sum is predicted to be £124.8 million in 2025.

But on top of this and entirely originating, like the Crown Estate, from William's victory at Hastings is the income King Charles receives from the Duchy of Lancaster, a huge estate of land and other property that produced £27 million income for the king in 2023/24. The Duchy of Cornwall produced similar profits for William, Prince of Wales.

Apart from these monies – from estates that cannot be sold – King Charles's private wealth is estimated at somewhere between £600 million (according to the most recent *Sunday Times* Rich List) and £1.8 billion (according to *The Guardian* newspaper). His private investment portfolio even includes rental property in Transylvania.

Given this extraordinary medieval level of wealth, is it any wonder Charles and other members of the royal family employ hundreds of gillies, gardeners, footmen, press officials, bag carriers, butlers, maids, stable hands, grooms, nannies, equerries, private assistants, secretaries and chauffeurs?

Land was always the key to power and prestige, and land was William I's to give or withhold. With the land ownership came peasant ownership: all the villeins who lived on the newly conquered land provided the lower servants for the new lords in their soon-to-be-built castles. Britain's richest landowner, the 7th Duke of Westminster, would not be Britain's richest landowner today if his ancestor who fought alongside William at Hastings had not been gifted a huge chunk of the newly conquered country by his friend the king. Westminster's wealth, like that of the monarchy, is effectively the spoils of war writ large.

The pattern of land ownership we see in Britain today still echoes the gifts of land given to his favourites by William I, but until relatively recently the land held by the nobility could be and occasionally was confiscated from even the greatest nobles.

Aristocrats stayed close to the monarch, advising and entertaining him, mostly to ensure he (or she) remained convinced of their loyalty. The monarch controlled, effectively owned, his nobles; the nobles in turn controlled, indeed owned, those who lived on the lands they were given by the king. The nobles were kept in check by the threat of violence and the ordinary people were kept in check by the same means.

No one should think for a minute that the knowledge that the royal family's wealth has come to them simply through an ancient act of war lessens the ruthlessness with which the Duchies of Lancaster and Cornwall are now managed. Royal wealth gained and held by the threat of violence in medieval times is now held and managed using the law and the threat of legal action. When, for example, Bristol City Council wanted to build a footbridge over the river Avon for the use of local citizens, the Crown Estate demanded more than £117,000 as its fee for what was described as an 'air-space levy'. The original fee demanded was £300,000, but after years of legal argument it was reduced. The fee was charged because since the conquest the monarch has owned the riverbed!

The execution of Charles I established that the monarch did not have absolute rights and absolute power; that land and property could no longer be appropriated at the whim of the monarch. As time passed, we came to believe that the great traditional landowners – the Dukes of Bedford, Westminster, Atholl and Beaufort, among many others – had somehow earned their wealth and land. In fact, they had simply hung on to what had been given them by one violent king or another; they had hung on into an age when there was no danger they might lose their land by the very means with which they took possession of it in the first place – currying favour.

I mention all this simply to drive home the point that for centuries everyone was a servant because everyone feared their livelihoods and status – and land – might vanish in an instant if they displeased the monarch. Monarchs were happy to be loved – both by their aristocratic servants and by those lower down the social scale – but they preferred to be feared. And as the nobility feared the violence of their master the king, so too did the peasantry fear their overlords. Only the small merchant class in medieval England seem to have escaped some aspects of the crushing power of the violence of hierarchy; certainly, they were subject to the crown, but they were not owned in the way the villeins were owned, nor were they subject to the whims of the monarch in the same way as the aristocrats. Their wealth came from trade, not land, and monarchs have always been careful not to interfere with trade since the wealth of a nation depends on it. When William the Conqueror defeated Harold and took control and ownership of England, he gave his followers land, but he didn't hand the City of London over in a similar way; instead, he sold it back to the merchants who had created and maintained its wealth. It was an acknowledgement that, small in number though they might be, the London merchants were somehow different.

* * *

Geneticists tell us that human faces, like all ape faces, have evolved to be flat, relative to most other mammals, because apes are violent, quarrelsome creatures that fight continually. If you have a flat face and you fight not by biting but by punching, you are less likely to suffer a serious facial injury in a fight compared to a mammal with a snout. As human societies evolved, fighting became ritualised and organised but no less frequent. According to Chris Hedges, writing in the *New York Times* in 2003, the best guess is that 'of the past 3,400 years, humans have been entirely at peace for 268 of them, or just 8 percent of recorded history'.

Through war and conquest, both external and internal, all

human societies have worked out some sort of hierarchy and just as ape societies establish hierarchies through violence, so too human hierarchies are or were originally established on the basis that might is effectively always right; the biggest, toughest ape is always at the top. Even today when there is a coup in a particular country it is often the head of the military – the biggest ape – who takes over.

I make this point at some length because traditional monarchies are rather similar, with the most powerful individual at the top by right of birth and everyone below that individual subservient to him or her. Before modern democracy in England, might always made right, which is why at Bosworth Field, in 1485, for example, Henry Tudor was able to kill Richard III and become top dog (or top ape) with absolute power over everyone from the greatest earl to the lowliest ploughman. No one has ever felt sorry for Richard, because he would have killed Henry just as readily as Henry killed him. In this case, as so often in battles between rivals for a throne, might made right and the winner took everything.

If we go back much further to discover the origins of monarchy (and the origins of royal servants), we can safely assume that violence lies close to its heart.

Archaeological evidence strongly suggests early farming communities in England and Europe made their own decisions about how to live in what were often remote, isolated areas. Squabbles and fights no doubt there were and the toughest and most persuasive no doubt usually got their way, but this was small-scale stuff.

Then came bands of armed knights – in *The Time Traveller's Guide to Medieval England*, Ian Mortimer refers to them as 'brigands' – who laid claim to large tracts of land that included many small, formerly self-governing farming communities. The knights told the farmers that all the land they farmed and lived on was now owned by the knights and that they would kill anyone who disagreed. For a more recent example we need look only to Australia, where Captain Cook planted the British flag in 1770 and claimed the whole of the island continent for George III. Behind the claim was the knowledge that the indigenous people did not have anything like the might of the British crown to dispute the assertion. Australia today is run by the descendants of Europeans because those Europeans were better at killing the original inhabitants than the original inhabitants were at killing the Europeans.

Ancient isolated farming communities were subdued by force and the knights – the brigands, or criminals, if you like – made themselves overlords, a situation that in many ways continues to this day, especially if one believes the old dictum that property is nine-tenths of the law. When the brigands took control of the land, they took control of people on the land.

But the knights were in turn eventually controlled by a more powerful force as one among them became first among equals and then, to use a phrase made famous by George Orwell, some found themselves to be more equal than others and thus were kings gradually established as overlords of the overlords.

But what has all this to do with the lives of royal servants, you may ask? Well, in a sense all royal servants, from the lowliest kitchen maid to the most aristocratic courier, are descended from servants and aristocratic companions whose roles were fixed a thousand years ago. And though the threat of violence has largely vanished from these relationships, the social gulf between maids and monarchs, lords and earls remains.

By the later medieval period, almost everyone worked for the monarch or the nobility. The land the common people worked was owned by the local lord, who would take a percentage of their produce each year. They could never own their land, they had a duty to fight for their lord if he went to war and, as Ian Mortimer points out, their masters had control not just of the lives of the villeins but also of their bodies. If a villein's daughter married a peasant owned by a neighbouring lord, the girl's father had to pay his master not just for the loss of the daughter but also for the loss of the children that daughter would be assumed to produce. This may seem extraordinary today, but then universal human rights are both a social construct and a very recent phenomenon.

And if the landowner wanted to rape a female peasant, it was simply accepted that he had the right to do it. In a diluted form, this kind of power – the power of master over servant – survived as late as the early twentieth century. In her 2012 memoir *The Maid's Tale*, former maid Rose Plummer's account of her days in service, she recalls how aristocratic employers saw the sexual harassment of female staff, some as young as twelve, as perfectly acceptable.

Aristocrats and the royal family have only very recently come to terms with the idea that their servants are entitled to their own lives. But even though formally no longer serfs and villeins, royal servants have been subjected to an informal yet powerful pressure emanating from the unthinking assumption that royal needs must come first.

When Marion Crawford told Queen Mary she wanted to leave to get married after twenty years of royal service, for example, Queen Mary was indignant. She told Crawford that it was quite impossible and asked how on earth Crawford expected the Princesses Elizabeth and Margaret to manage on their own. Not one word about Crawford, her life, her desire to marry or her future husband. Lower down the social scale, the same assumptions persisted: in his semi-autobiographical novel *Buddenbrooks*, Thomas Mann explains how it was simply assumed in the family that Ide Jungmann, their servant, would work for the family, without marrying or having children, until she died.

Royalty and the aristocracy have always resisted reforms to the way they manage their estates and their servants – as late as 1909, the House of Lords, at that time overwhelmingly dominated by hereditary peers, rejected the idea that a small basic pension should be introduced by the government for the poor. Hereditary peers at the time insisted that *they* would provide for their pensioned-off estate workers – but only if they chose to do so.

* * *

I argue in this book that royal servants are in many ways the direct descendants of the villeins, the slaves, who worked without pay and without rights for those medieval kings and their brigand aristocrats. Gradually, societal changes – most especially the execution of Charles I, which destroyed the idea that the monarch could do as he pleased – led to former serfs and slaves being paid and enjoying limited and then gradually evolving rights, but at least until the twentieth century most of those rights taken from the monarch were taken in order to protect the privileges not of the servant classes but of the nobility.

Royal servants have always been part of the endless battles for power. If you could kill a king, you could become one. But then you needed the safety of loyal retainers to ensure you kept what you had taken. After Henry VII killed Richard III at Bosworth, he knew his hold on the crown and his right to that crown were shaky. To protect his weak position, he made sure the servants with whom he surrounded himself were not drawn, as they traditionally would have been, from the upper echelons of the aristocracy. That was too dangerous, as the nobles might have done to him what he had done to Richard III. So, for Henry VII's reign the gentry found themselves in elevated courtier positions previously held only by the aristocracy. Instead of being an earl or a lord, Henry's Groom of the Stool, for example, was Hugh Denys, the son of a Gloucestershire farmer.

* * *

'They also serve who only stand and wait' – that famous phrase from John Milton fits nicely with the theme of this book, because according to many former and serving royals servants I've spoken to there is an awful lot of hanging around when you work for the royal family.

But while they are standing around, or fetching or carrying, advising or comforting their royal masters, royal servants (or staff as we must now call them) are more aware than anyone of what really goes in in the royal palaces: they see at first hand the squabbles and petty jealousies, the arguments and tantrums that inevitably take place in what is by any standards one of the strangest families in the world. And royal staff frequently have unique insights because they are descended, in some cases quite literally, from those early villeins and flattering nobles; that they are expected to have a higher level of devotion to their work and their masters than staff who work for other families is entirely a legacy of the old order examined in the previous chapter.

Royal staff may in some senses still be treated like serfs, but they are also acutely aware of the upside of working for the royals in the twenty-first century. The royal family is so nervous of criticism that staff are now treated very well – although salaries are still often poor – and modern royals at least attempt to put on a more human face. It is too easy to assume that the royals are invariably dull, serious, demanding and unkind both to each other and to the people who work for them. That is sometimes true but by no means always – as a member of the Kensington Palace staff explained to me:

They [the senior royals] can be really light-hearted and jokey with each other – the late Queen and Prince Philip were a hoot.

Occasionally, I had to ask to be excused before breaking down in fits of giggles. I once forgot myself in front of them and almost dropped a valuable plate. I instinctively mumbled, 'Oh shit.' The Queen spluttered as she started to laugh and said, 'Well, quite.'

The key point is that royal service is still somehow special; royal staff certainly don't see themselves as serfs but they are expected to be highly discreet – highly secretive – and to see working for the royals as somehow a special privilege. In this sense, royal staff echo the ancient idea of serfdom in which service to a noble or a king is seen as its own reward.

Many royal staff endure long hours for little pay, sometimes for the whole of their working lives, simply because they are so dazzled by the idea that they are working for the royal family, even if they are only in the kitchen. And there is still an obsession with social hierarchy in royal service – an obsession that would not be unfamiliar to royal staff 600 years ago.

Senior staff, especially courtiers, are still mostly aristocrats or at least public school educated; in some cases, they are descended from families that have worked for the royal family for centuries – the Keppels, and the Dukes of Norfolk, for example. Courtiers do not see the kitchen staff as their equals – one courtier I spoke to about the vastly different salaries of aristocratic staff compared to domestic staff said, 'You see, they simply don't need a great deal of money – after all, they don't need to pay school fees as we do.'

* * *

It is difficult to imagine now, but servants have always been just as snobbish as their employers, perhaps even more so. Only the inexperienced or desperate would work in a small household with one or two servants; the aim was to work for the nobility at least, and that was often seen as a stepping stone to the ultimate in servant status – the royal family.

But if a servant couldn't quite make the royal family, he would do almost anything to escape working in a middle-class household. A valet describing his life in *Toilers in London*, published in 1889, said, 'It's only the aristocracy who treat servants properly … The aristocracy know how to behave to a gentleman even if he happens to be a servant.'

It's easy to think everything in the nineteenth and early twentieth centuries – perhaps the heyday of servant life – was serious and worthy, rather as we think of that world as monochrome simply because photographs and film from the time are black and white. There *was* colour and there *was* fun and surprisingly that was especially true in the royal family. The middle classes, always worried about their status, felt it was proper and more refined to be harsh with their staff; the royals, by contrast, often treated their servants extremely well. The late Queen Elizabeth II loved joking with her staff – standing next to one of her security team on one famous occasion outside the gates of Balmoral, she was asked by a passer-by (who clearly had no inkling who this tiny woman in a headscarf was) if she had met the Queen. Without a flicker, the Queen replied, 'No, but he has.' At which she pointed to her security detail.

Similar examples are legion and I have one from my own

experience. I was allowed to be part of a small group surrounding Queen Elizabeth at a large country show; I'd been given special permission to join her entourage as she had heard I was there on behalf of one of her favourite magazines. Unfortunately, her security detail did not seem to be aware of my special permission and I suddenly found myself unceremoniously manhandled away from the Queen. The Queen stepped across to where I was being dragged away and said, 'He really isn't a rabbit to be picked up by the scruff of the neck, you know. I think you can safely put him down. He looks fairly harmless.' And with that I was released with a grudging apology from a very fierce-looking but rather small (and absurdly well-spoken) security man. As we continued on our way, with the Queen herself a yard or two ahead, I asked my assailant if he had to carry interlopers off frequently. 'Secrets of the trade,' he replied. 'Happens all the time. Most people who get too close are harmless, but you never know – it's the little old ladies that worry me. I can boot you over a hedge, but I can't do that to Mrs Warren aged eighty from Tunbridge Wells who might be angry with the Queen for some unknown eccentric reason and want to whack her with an umbrella. And I can tell you, I've had to deal with the umbrella brigade a few times.'

* * *

Most of the major changes that have transpired in the way royal servants are treated occurred during the reign of Queen Elizabeth II. Earlier generations had not felt the wind of egalitarianism blowing as Elizabeth did. Queen Mary, her grandmother, disliked ever seeing any of the lower servants bustling about her various palaces, and a strict regime ensured that cleaning and cooking went on well out of her sight, but then she had grown up in an age when lower servants were seen as a necessary evil.

Nigel Nicolson, son of the writer and socialite Vita Sackville-West, recalled how his mother stepped over a servant cleaning the front doorstep on her hands and knees as if the cleaner were something that might have soiled his mother's footwear. And this was typical of the royal and aristocratic view of their own elevated status and the lowly status of those who worked for them. Vita Sackville-West's family were the owners of Knole in Kent – a vast medieval house – and her great-grandfather was the 5th Earl De La Warr, Lord Chamberlain of the Royal Household to Queen Victoria.

Queen Elizabeth II grew up in this world, but unlike many, she sensed how things were gradually changing. Perhaps she recognised early on that by the end of her reign, treating staff in any way that suggested they were inferior would no longer be acceptable, but there is some evidence that even back in the 1930s, when Elizabeth was a girl, she treated all her more intimate staff with respect and affection.

It has been noted by a number of royal watchers – including the present writer – that the royal family actually feels far more comfortable with the traditional working classes than they feel with the nouveau riche and the aspiring middle classes. The problem with the English middle classes for the royals was always their lack of certainty about their social position. As one royal servant explained to the present author:

Queen Elizabeth liked the ordinary girls in the kitchen, the ordinary soldiers and footmen and gardeners and she liked the toffs – people like her best friend Porchey – but she didn't feel comfortable with grammar school boys, middle-class boys who had done well at school and in life. She thought they were never comfortable in their own shoes – she thought they were a bit chippy. You know, had chips on their shoulders about their origins. The Porchies and Norfolks who had gone to Eton and Harrow for generations – she just felt more comfortable with them because they never worried about their social position. And the working classes for her were the same.

No working-class cockney would ever claim to have been at Eton, but thousands of middle-class men have claimed to be Old Etonians, such is the desperation among the middle classes to seem upper middle class or even aristocratic. In a conversation with the present author, a retired member of the Eton staff said, 'I sometimes think more living people claim to have been at Eton than have attended the school in its whole history!'

The awkwardness of not knowing quite where to place someone socially has always made the royal family more comfortable with servants who know their place – staff are either from grand backgrounds or they have no pretensions at all to grandeur. Best of all are those families that have always provided courtiers and aristocratic companions: the Earls of Albemarle have worked for the royal family since the seventeenth century, for example. With these people the royals feel at home, but for entirely opposite reasons the same is true of their footmen and maids, their keepers and drivers, gillies and personal assistants.

Of course, it is not a universal truth – some royals, notably Prince Andrew, have earned a reputation for being overbearing, occasionally short-tempered and imperious, even rude, to their staff, in what might be described as a traditional but deeply dated attitude – but King Charles and Queen Camilla always treat their staff carefully if not well. One former member of their staff explained to the present author:

Charles and Camilla do treat their staff well, but you always feel that they would no more fly without an aeroplane than invite you to have tea with them. And Charles does have little bursts of irritation with his staff – perhaps he hasn't been given exactly the right teacup, perfectly polished shoes and toothpaste neatly squeezed on to his toothbrush in exactly the way he likes it. He loses his temper in a split second but usually quickly regrets it.

Andrew often behaved as if his staff were irritatingly stupid and this was particularly true with his little quirks – famously, he has his collection of teddy bears lined up in order on his bed every day and if anything is out of place he loses his temper. So much so that a particular maid was assigned each day to arrange the teddies because she tended to get it right and Andrew liked her.

But all members of the royal family are very good at talking to each other and their friends in front of servants as if the servants just aren't there. It looks like rudeness, but really it isn't – the royals are the last family, possibly on earth, who sometimes see the servants as furniture. This was a universal thing among the aristocracy in earlier times, but only the royal family has retained the ability. It comes from growing up surrounded by people who will do anything, however silly or trivial, that you ask them to do.

Charles confessed to another member of staff that if you grow up having everything done for you, a mindset takes over in which you are permanently terrified that if you had to do it yourself, you'd be completely lost. If you grow up with staff, you simply assume that all your needs will be catered for. He said, 'It's the only benefit of being Prince of Wales [as Charles then was] twenty-four hours a day and seven days a week.'

One of Charles's former equerries said, 'Oligarchs and the newly rich might believe that treating their staff as inferiors proves their elevated status, but senior royals know that, today, the opposite is generally true.'

True nobility might best be illustrated using what has now become an almost apocryphal tale attributed to Queen Victoria, as well as to Baron Kilmarnock and at least three other aristocrats. At lunch with a group of guests that included one or two from very different backgrounds than her own, the story goes, the Queen (or Kilmarnock!) noticed that, unsure what to do with his finger bowl, one guest lifted it to his lips and drank. She immediately lifted her bowl and drank to avoid embarrassing the guest. Every other diner followed suit.

Trying to make 'inferiors' feel less uncomfortable is definitely part of the modern royal ethos, but outsiders are often astonished at how few of their daily tasks the royals do for themselves.

A former maid who worked at Kensington Palace said:

One of the royal princes – I mean Elizabeth II's sons (and I'm not saying which one) – used to make me disinfect the telephone receiver every day while holding it with a sterile cloth. Another prince – again, I'm not saying who – used to say, 'Clear the decks', which meant I had to scurry out of the room and make sure no staff were loitering between the prince and the lavatory he was planning to visit. The same prince would not allow staff with moles on their faces to work for him. He also liked to throw things around – bouncing a tennis ball off the walls and catching it – with the result that expensive clocks and ornaments were constantly getting broken, and they must have cost a fortune to mend. They were always mended without anyone saying anything or asking the prince to stop his games.

From looking down on their staff and pretending they were not there, members of the royal family have, generally speaking, come full circle. They have learned to enjoy their staff and the fact that they are lucky enough to have staff; staff reciprocate in many cases and see their royal employers at their most relaxed and informal.

Of course, even the nicest royals become irritated with their staff occasionally and some royals are nicer than others; what we might call the also-rans, royals such as Princess Margaret and Prince Andrew, tend to be more imperious with their staff in proportion to their own relative lack of status.

Being close to the senior royals, whatever your own social

class, always meant there was a slim chance that for some entirely unpredictable reason one might catch the monarch's eye. The wealth and status enjoyed by the Earls of Albemarle today is entirely based on the fact that William III spotted a handsome young man during a hunting outing and brought him to London, and not for entirely altruistic reasons. Likewise the Dukes of St Albans; their wealth and status stem from the fact that Charles II took a fancy to an illiterate but very pretty orange seller plying her trade in London's Haymarket. That orange seller was of course Nell Gwynne, whose son Charles – the son of Charles II – was made an earl aged fourteen.

So just being close to the monarch – even if in the kitchens – always meant a chance of preferment. One former Balmoral maid interviewed by the present author confessed that meeting the Queen was 'like meeting a Hollywood star, but so much better. It took me a year to get over it, even though I worked in the same house where the Queen spent every summer.'

Working for the royals occasionally produces servants who become so devoted to their royal masters that they work twenty-four hours a day and seven days a week caring very little about free time or their own lives. So dazzled are they by their proximity to royalty that they give up everything to spend every possible moment in the service of their royal masters.

We see this reflected in literature. When the Duke of Kent is banished by King Lear in Shakespeare's eponymous play, for giving advice the king does not want to hear, he disguises himself, determined to continue to serve his master. Just before he is banished by the king on pain of death, he says:

My life I never held but as a pawn
To wage against thine enemies, nor fear to lose it,
Thy safety being motive.

William Tallon – better known as Backstairs Billy – who was the late Queen Elizabeth, the Queen Mother's obsessively loyal servant for more than fifty years would have understood this level of loyalty, as would Bobo MacDonald, Queen Elizabeth II's nanny and later dresser.

Shortly before Bobo MacDonald's death in 1993, I interviewed a former member of the Buckingham Palace staff, someone who knew her well. She said:

Bobo would have quite happily died for the Queen. Devotion is not the word; it was a kind of feudal loyalty. She had known the Queen since the Queen was a toddler. She had never married, never lived away from Elizabeth, and she once said to me, 'I never regretted not having my own children. I can't explain it other than to say I loved Lillibet as much as any parent could love their own child. She was my child in all but the biological sense. I had looked after her day and night throughout her childhood because her parents were always away, always busy.

Queen Elizabeth used to insist, jokingly, that her love of horse racing stemmed from the fun she'd had as a toddler being given endless piggybacks by Bobo.

But this level of devotion was far more common in earlier centuries because in days gone by, having found a job in royal service there was nowhere higher or more prestigious to go, whether you were a commoner or a member of the nobility. It was a question of glitter by association. Being in royal service even as a lowly maid or groom could bring not just a sense of profound purpose – the purpose felt by Bobo MacDonald – but practical benefits: gifts and preferment both for oneself and for one's family.

We need to remember too that in earlier centuries royalty had vastly more staff than they have employed in the modern era. And despite our conviction that social mobility is a modern phenomenon, we should remember that in royal circles, even three or four hundred years ago, ability could enable you to rise to the top. Thomas Cromwell is a good example: his father owned a pub in Putney and may also have worked as a blacksmith. Hardly an auspicious beginning and yet Cromwell rose to be Lord Privy Seal and Chancellor of the Exchequer. Cromwell's life is exceptional but not unique.

Chapter Three

The gentleman's gentleman: butlers, valets and footmen

'I had such an awful afternoon with my bank manager scolding me about my overdraft.'
– Queen Elizabeth, the Queen Mother

'If you are not born into royalty, you never really belong.'
– Sarah, Duchess of York

The role of butler is a curious one. In medieval England it denoted the servant who looked after a nobleman's wine; indeed, according to the *Oxford English Dictionary*, the word 'butler' comes from the Norman French *butelier*, meaning the official in charge of the king's wine – and from which the modern word 'bottle' is also derived. At a time when wine was expensive, this was a coveted and highly responsible job, and yet it was never a job given to a nobleman. The preparation of food and the serving of wine were and always have been seen by royalty as relatively menial tasks, despite the importance of food and drink.

Households able to afford a butler have always been a cut above the rest, but in the royal household the butler was never the most senior servant. He was outranked by the house steward, who in turn reported to the comptroller of the royal household, a neat way of making sure that, ultimately, a nobleman rather than a commoner was in charge. Comptrollers have always been aristocrats, though in reality the comptroller is little more than a souped-up servant in charge of all the other servants and with responsibility for how the royal household is run.

Like most very senior royal jobs, the comptroller's is rather vague – partly, one suspects, to make sure no one could ever actually accuse the comptroller of getting his hands dirty. Not so the butler, whose role has become synonymous with aristocratic living. Popular culture through novels and television programmes has turned the butler into an archetype: the butler epitomises the dignified servant who behaves to visitors and strangers with as much if not more hauteur than the aristocrat (or royal) for whom he works.

But fictional portrayals of butlers also develop the idea that those who employ them are often too stupid to do anything for themselves. In J. M. Barrie's 1902 play *The Admirable Crichton*, for example, an aristocratic family is shipwrecked on a remote island. Having never looked after themselves, they become entirely reliant on their practical butler for survival. Slowly he takes the place of the former head of the family, who is useless in this new environment. P. G. Wodehouse's stories of Jeeves and Wooster make a similar though less serious point – Jeeves the socially inferior butler is actually far more intelligent and capable than his dim-witted master.

In an interview with the present author in 1998, a former member of the Buckingham Palace staff said:

> The senior royals including Queen Elizabeth [the Queen Mother] sometimes got irritated if they didn't like the advice of their staff and they would say, 'Now we know how Bertie felt,' meaning Bertie Wooster, who you may remember was always given slightly patronising advice by his far more intelligent servant, the butler Jeeves.

Butlers have always been male – originally, of course, this was because a large intimidating man was more likely to be able to fend off thieves trying to get at the royal wine cellars, and before water was safe to drink, wine was a scarce, expensive and highly valued commodity that needed to be protected by a servant who could be trusted absolutely.

In a nobleman's house, the butler might be the most senior servant for the indoor staff, but the definitions of the different jobs varied enormously over time and from house to house, depending often on the number of servants that could be afforded. In the royal family, staff roles existed that could not be found anywhere else.

We can discover something of this range of tasks in a long-forgotten book published in the early 1890s. The book, *The Private Life of the Queen*, was written, according to the title page, by 'One of her Majesty's Servants'. The anonymous author tells us that at Windsor Castle there were 'two pantries, in reality strong rooms, separated by two plate cleaning rooms'. So, virtually a fortress, and here a 'yeoman of the pantries' was employed full-time just cleaning plates and delivering them to the dining room or banqueting room. The yeoman of the pantries was undoubtedly unique to palace life, but creating new titles for servants was just an additional means by which the royal family could make sure everyone was aware that their status meant they could afford more servants than anyone else.

The proliferation of servant titles in many ways parallels the proliferation of equipment – as one former palace servant explained in an interview with the present author in 1988.

It was ridiculous – as well as sugar tongs and grape scissors we had skirting board brushes, wall brushes, carpet frill combs, spoon heaters and egg warmers made of wool. There were special small silver knives for peeling apples, and any little tool or implement that was part of a place setting at table had to be pure silver or gold and delicate. In the kitchens we had equivalent tools but they were crude versions, made of steel or pewter. It was ridiculous, really, and created far more washing up than was necessary. In my grandmother's time at the palace, all the grease had to be got off the knives and forks using brick dust and vinegar, so you needed huge numbers of kitchen maids – and everyone knew a kitchen maid, even a royal one, by the terrible state of their hands!

Servant status was complicated. As Frank Huggett points out in

Life Below Stairs, published in 1977, many very grand houses employed a groom of the chambers, who outranked both the valet and the butler. He was a sort of super-butler – but in the royal household, he in turn would be outranked by the comptroller. But butlers were still important because they oversaw banquets and luncheons and ensured that the footmen and other male domestic staff did their jobs properly. The king's valet was not under the control of the butler (which often caused friction), just as the queen's personal servants and lady's maid were not answerable to the housekeeper, who was in charge of all the other below-stairs female staff. Adding to the confusion is the fact that the comptroller – always, remember, a man – was in overall charge of everything to do with the servants.

Valets might slowly become close to their royal masters, since they were intimately involved with their day-to-day lives, but this was rarely so with the butler, although the late Diana Spencer's butler Paul Burrell seems to be an exception. After the publication of his book about working for the Princess of Wales, Burrell was accused of exaggerating his closeness to the princess, but regardless of the truth or otherwise of this charge, various royal staff jobs have lost much of their original strict demarcation. Burrell might be seen as a latter-day John Brown, who we may recall became so close to Queen Victoria that it was rumoured they were lovers.

Angela Kelly, the late Queen Elizabeth II's dresser, was never quite that close to her mistress, but where a queen's dresser might once have actually dressed the Queen each day, Kelly was employed instead to design and choose the Queen's outfits. The person who helped Elizabeth dress each day was in fact Margaret 'Bobo' MacDonald, who, as we have seen, was first nursery-maid and nanny to the child princess and later one of her closest friends. This may have represented a change, but it wasn't such a revolutionary change to the old order – there was no chance, for example, that Bobo might become a lady in waiting. As a former member of the Buckingham Palace staff explained in an interview with the present author:

> Elizabeth loved Bobo, was devoted to her in many ways, but would have been the first to agree that Bobo was not a lady. Elizabeth had unquestioningly absorbed the values of her ancestors and these values included the deep and unchanging assumption that a lady is by definition of noble birth. Bobo was not of noble birth, so she was not a lady. Simple. And Bobo knew and accepted it. But it's complicated because Elizabeth often preferred her non-noble staff to the aristocratic women who surrounded her early in her reign. I once heard her say about a particular lady in waiting, 'Of course she's one of my oldest friends, but one's oldest friends are not always much fun.'

Paul Burrell may have become an emotional support for Diana, but butlers have been asked over the centuries to be that and a great deal more.

According to Nancy Jackman, whose memoir *The Cook's Tale* was published in 2012, a cousin of the late Queen insisted that her butler dance with her each evening when she was at home.

She told him that if he mentioned what they were doing, he would be dismissed without a reference.

The work of the butler still demands discretion, but it has glamorous elements – Grant Harrold, formerly butler to King Charles III, has set himself up as an expert on etiquette, as no doubt he is. Such a move for a retired butler in earlier times would have been seriously frowned upon. When 'one of her majesty's servants' published a book on the private life of Queen Victoria, quoted above, the book was quickly suppressed and all unsold copies destroyed in 1897 after a furious response from the monarch. Today, Mr Harrold would quite rightly be as indignant as Victoria if he were told he could not benefit from his experience as a royal butler.

Butlers have always thought highly of themselves, and with good reason, because traditionally they ruled the below-stairs staff, and often with a rod of iron. The lower servants not only had to obey their butler masters; they also had to wait on them at table, just as they had to wait on members of the royal family. Albert Thomas, a former servant who published *Wait and See* in 1934, described how at least once a week he was forced to wash the feet of the Duke of Norfolk's butler.

A former royal butler interviewed by the present author in 1995 insisted that, being in charge of the wine cellar, very few butlers were able to resist the temptation of drink.

Well, think about it – you are not very well paid and in the royal palaces you are not top dog, but you have access to hundreds if not thousands of bottles of the finest wines. You start by having the odd sip to cheer you up on a busy, stressful day and before you know it you are drinking a bottle or two a day. No one will ever notice because all the royal palaces have cellars absolutely crammed with wines, some very rare and expensive. I loved drinking the royal wines. Far more enjoyable than any other aspect of the job, so long as you were fairly sober during banquets and dinners, when you had to be on your best behaviour.

Edward VII would never notice if you were drunk because he was almost always drunk himself, and George V and George VI liked a few drinks too, although they were moderate drinkers really. But the point is they would have thought it beneath them to ask the comptroller to check the butler wasn't helping himself [to the wine]. It was a culture they grew up in and a clever butler knew just how far he could go.

One of the most famous of all royal servants, William Tallon, dubbed Backstairs Billy by the newspapers, was never employed as a butler, but he was so trusted that he regularly ordered wine for himself and his friends and charged it to the Queen Mother's account. A friend of William's explained to the author:

The Queen Mother probably knew what William was doing, but she didn't mind a bit. She had no idea it was costing her a great deal of money, but on the other hand she was so dotty in many ways that she assumed everything supplied to Clarence House was supplied free of charge.

Royal servants have always helped themselves to supplement their incomes. Chris Leventon worked in the kitchens at Buckingham Palace in the 1970s and in an interview with the present author he said:

> The lower staff, the drudges in the kitchen particularly, often stole spoons and forks or bits of linen – often just as trophies – and the senior staff definitely knew it was going on. The butler would never have caught us because the kitchens were huge and with so many staff rushing here and there, how could anyone really keep an eye on things fully? I used to think in fact that a certain amount of stealing was allowed for and accepted grudgingly. If people stole to supplement their incomes, the comptroller of the household knew he could get away with paying very low wages.

Similar problems have always existed and for similar reasons. In his 2018 study, *Behind the Throne*, Adrian Tinniswood recalls the sensational mid-nineteenth-century trial of sisters Ellen and Lizzie Lindsay for stealing sheets and other items of linen from Buckingham Palace. The sisters, who had worked as maids at the palace, were acquitted because the jury heard from a string of royal servants that the palace organisation was completely chaotic and no one could keep track of anything.

Butlers were supposed to stop this kind of thing happening, but as the social world they and the royals inhabited changed in the twentieth century, the strict below-stairs hierarchical system began to break down and chaos to some extent became the norm. Suddenly, just as the royals could no longer treat their staff as if they were just useful bits of furniture, so too the senior staff could no long treat the maids and boot boys as if they were scarcely human.

In earlier times, butlers had tended to treat the lower staff harshly because they had themselves started at the bottom and been badly treated. It was a system rather like fagging at public school – boys whipped when they were junior fags turned into enthusiastic whippers of their own juniors as they moved up through the school.

Butlers usually began their careers in the royal household as footmen or as junior assistants – a junior assistant was essentially a dogsbody – and just as the role of the butler gradually changed, so too did the role and function of the footman.

One major change dispensed completely with the work of a very particular kind of footman: the running footman. Queen Victoria hated reducing her staff or rationalising the way the royal household was run. From her earliest years, she had taken it for granted that she should be surrounded by servants who were often employed to do things that were entirely unnecessary. They were there to show that the royal family was above all other families in being able to employ servants to stand around doing nothing. As a child, Victoria had grown used to this sort of thing. Writing in *Old Court Suburb*, published in 1855, Leigh Hunt recalled, 'I saw her [Princess Victoria] coming up a cross path from the Bayswater Gate [in Kensington Gardens] with a girl of her own age by her side … Behind her came a magnificent footman in scarlet.'

But there were limits. When she insisted that she be allowed to employ what was called a running footman, her advisers thought she had gone too far. It was explained to her, as Frank Huggett recalls in *Life Below Stairs*, that employing a running footman would not make her more popular with her subjects and was highly likely to make her far less popular, as the general view – and it was one that was not entirely unfair – was that she was recklessly extravagant.

Victoria's predecessors had always employed a running footman and although she gave way on the subject, she was not happy. Just as she insisted on retaining her hereditary falconer, despite owning no falcons, she felt a running footman was essential not for practical reasons but for reasons of status. Just like a medieval monarch, she thought that as there was no limit to her importance, so there should be no limit to her spending.

But what was a running footman? Well, he was a poor devil employed to run in front of the royal carriage carrying a long staff fitted at one end with a large silver ball. Inside the ball was a supply of brandy, as even royalty recognised that without something to buoy him up, a running footman might collapse halfway through a journey, especially as at least for journeys across London he was expected to run the whole distance, which might be as far as eight or ten miles.

Frank Huggett repeats a wonderful story about a relative of Victoria's who advertised for a running footman. He chose a likely-looking young man and set off with his new hire racing ahead of the carriage carrying his freshly acquired silver-topped staff – but when the carriage stopped for a short time in the press of traffic, the young man kept running and neither he nor the silver-topped cane were ever seen again.

Footmen of all types were not always so lucky and protocol often demanded that they become almost anonymous. Victoria, like all monarchs until recent times, insisted that a lady's first footman should always be known as James, regardless of his actual name.

Changing names in this way was common in the royal household. In her memoir *The Cook's Tale*, Nancy Jackman remembered how footmen and other male servants with what were perceived as 'overly refined names' were always renamed by palace officials.

I remember a very elderly woman who had long retired from royal service telling me that when she was young, towards the end of Victoria's reign, a young man was taken on as a junior footman. He was tall and good looking – essential back then if you were to be accepted as a footman to the royal family – but there was a huge problem. He was called Albert. The senior staff told him he could not possibly use that name, as the Queen would be furious to hear that a lowly servant was to be addressed by the same name with which she had once addressed her husband. So the poor footman became William and was told he would be dismissed if he mentioned his real name.

This renaming of servants to reduce the sense of their individuality was also a feature of aristocratic life and until recently even extended to the servants in top London clubs. In the Beefsteak Club (originally the Sublime Society of Beefsteaks), founded in

1735, all the waiters are still called Charles regardless of their real names. Partly, no doubt, this was to remove the difficulty that inebriated members might have remembering individual waiter's names, but the practice also reveals a great deal about how servants were not seen as individual human beings.

Perhaps the most intriguing aspect of the footman's role was that he was expected to have large, muscular calves. He must also be tall – strong legs and height were seen as essential, a legacy of the days when a team of footmen might have to carry a sedan chair. Even at the end of Victoria's reign and on into the twentieth century, height and muscular calves were still expected, though more for aesthetic than for practical reasons. If a young man was suitable for the role of footman but he lacked the necessary calves, servant outfitters stocked artificial calves, which were stuffed down the footman's stockings to make sure his calves appeared suitably burly.

For Victoria, a lady's footman was essential if she wanted to go for a walk, because the footman carried small sums of money in case she wanted to stop and buy something; there is no record of any of them ever absconding with the royal purse.

Just as earls preceded lords and lords preceded knights, so there were strict ranks among the footmen – the lady's footman had to be a paragon among footmen, the tallest and best looking and best behaved; below him were other footmen, who, though shorter and less good looking, might occasionally deputise for the first footman or lady's footman.

Within the world of male servants, perhaps the most bizarre fact – and it was a fact that reflected in miniature the huge discrimination between men and women – was that from 1777 until as recently as 1937, if you chose to employ a 'non-essential' male servant in any capacity, you had to pay a special tax for the privilege. And the word 'privilege' is key to the thinking behind the tax: it was a way of ensuring that only royalty or those just a rung or two below them could afford to employ male servants in any numbers. Employing female servants was relatively inexpensive – even people living in small suburban houses could afford a maid or two. But the tax on male servants ensured you had to be very grand indeed (and very wealthy indeed) to afford the ultimate sign of status – a team of male servants. And of course, top of the status pile was always the royal family, who employed vast numbers of male servants.

According to Frank Huggett's *Life Below Stairs*, the 'man tax', as it was known, was £7 per year per manservant when first introduced in the late eighteenth century; £7 was a great deal of money at that time (equivalent to almost £1,000 in 2024), so paying the tax for a whole fleet of manservants was far beyond the reach of all but the very wealthy.

The higher value placed on male servants both stemmed from and reinforced a view that they were not just status symbols but also somehow more reliable and more capable than women servants.

Queen Victoria much preferred her male servants and could be indulgent towards them in a way she never was with her female servants. In the anonymously published book *The Private Life of the Queen*, there is a marvellous story of a young, newly appointed equerry visiting the royal stables and coming across an old lady dressed in black and wearing a 'countrified black gown' and a 'mushroom hat'.

The author continues:

> Filled with the importance of his new dignity, the zealous official shouted across the intervening stalls, 'My good woman, you must get out of this! Strangers are not allowed here, especially when her majesty is in residence.'
>
> He finished his remarks by warning her that he would escort her to the gate himself if she was not quick in going. His feelings on discovering that the shabbily dressed intruder was his royal mistress in person may be better imagined than described, but the queen with delightful good humour forgave him and at the same time complimented him on his zeal and obedience to standing orders.

Had the young man been a young woman, the outcome would probably have been very different.

The story reveals a side of Victoria that reached its most extreme in her relationship with her gillie John Brown. Brown has been written about at length elsewhere, and portrayed on screen by Billy Connolly in the 1997 film *Mrs Brown*, but suffice to say his relationship with the queen was intense and according to Victoria's biographer A. N. Wilson probably led to some sort of secret marriage ceremony. According to Bendor Grosvenor, writing in *History Today* magazine in 2023, Brown's relationship with Victoria was more than platonic. He writes, 'The similarities between Victoria's treatment of Albert and Brown in death are too numerous to ignore.' Her own letters reveal the depths of her distress at Brown's passing; the queen also issued instructions that on her own death, mementoes including a lock of Brown's hair and a photograph should be placed in her coffin along with those of Albert.

We also have a letter from the Dean of Windsor expressing outrage that Brown was permitted to sleep at Windsor Castle in the room next to Victoria's own bedroom, 'contrary to etiquette and even decency'. Then there were Victoria's daughters' jokes about 'Mama's lover'; on a more serious level, her second son the Duke of Edinburgh was told by Victoria that he could no longer live at Buckingham Palace after refusing to shake Brown's hand.

A lot of this had to do with Victoria's desire for sex. Letters written in the weeks and months after her marriage to Albert reveal how much she enjoyed sex. Knowing she couldn't remarry after his death, she turned her physical attentions to senior male servants she could safely control: first Brown and later on Abdul Karim, her Indian servant.

The extent to which Victoria's children and palace officials hated all this can be judged by the fact that Victoria's eldest son had all Brown's statues and memorials either stored away or destroyed after his mother's death in 1901. And Abdul Karim was quietly – and very quickly – sent back to India.

What the queen loved in Brown was his brusqueness, his manliness. He scolded her, he told her off and pointed out her faults as no one else ever dared to and she loved it because it reminded her of Albert, with whom she had not had the doting relationship some would have us believe. The equerry in the stables, like John Brown and Albert, had a kind of no-nonsense masculinity for which the queen longed. Other male servants in other eras have entranced their royal mistresses and masters in similar ways.

The late Queen Mother once confessed to her favourite servant, the former footman and later page of the backstairs William Tallon, that 'girls are too frivolous and unintelligent to make senior servants'.

Footmen may have seen themselves as a cut above the rest – or at least a cut above all male servants except the butler, valets and the gentlemen attendants and advisers – but they still had to suffer various indignities as part of the job. Until well into the twentieth century royal footmen were forced to wear uncomfortable powdered, horsehair wigs, for example. Even Elizabeth II, who was careful to avoid anything too obviously sexist, insisted that a footman rather than a maid should always have the job of cleaning up after the corgis (who were allowed to pee on the carpets at Buckingham Palace).

Nancy Jackman's great-uncle had been a footman in the royal household and he remembered the discomfort of horsehair and powder. In her memoir, *The Cook's Tale*, she records him saying:

At the time I felt I was incredibly lucky to be working at the palace – I was so proud with my magnificent uniform – but looking back it was a sort of slavery. We had very little time off, the hours were very long and the wigs were so uncomfortable – horsehair is like bloody barbed wire … They judged footmen according to the way they judged furniture – you needed a well-turned leg, but the main skill was being able to look serious the whole time and to be in a real sense a piece of furniture. You spoke when you were spoken to and moved only when told to move. Being able to stay absolutely still for long periods was vital and for some reason we were not to smile – ever. I remember one poor lad was demoted because when the king was dining, he broke into a fit of giggles. The king [Edward VII] thought it was funny, but the senior members of the household decided the poor footman was not footman material and he was removed. But standing and waiting were not the only things we had to do – we had to polish the silver and in the case of royalty it was often not silver but solid gold.

Nancy's great-uncle would have been far more indignant a century earlier when, to save money, many of those who employed footmen substituted wheat flour for hair powder. There was a tax on hair powder and even the very rich tried to avoid paying it. In hot weather the wheat flour would become sticky and the poor footman would find that, eventually, his head was coated with a layer of something very much like glue.

All servants but perhaps especially footmen were expected to devote their lives to royal service. Footmen who married were seen as almost letting the side down. Footmen who did well and made it clear that they were happy to devote themselves to their masters often moved up to become valets – the position often known as the gentleman's gentleman.

The valet was the male equivalent to the lady's maid – they were servants, it is true, but their intimate work with kings and queens, princes and princesses elevated them far beyond the lowly kitchen staff.

A former Buckingham Palace maid who worked at the palace between the wars recalled how

> ladies' maids and valets, but especially valets, gave themselves airs and graces that matched those of their royal masters and mistresses. We kitchen staff accepted that we were a lower sort and always would be – if you had a cockney accent, there was no way a member of the royal family would allow you to become a lady's maid.

Valets and ladies' maids were the modern equivalent to the earlier roles of gentlemen and gentlewomen of the bedchamber. These latter titles still existed in the twentieth century, but they had become honorary titles and were given to the royals' aristocratic friends, who were no longer expected to help dress and wash their charges.

However elevated and important a valet or lady's maid might feel, there were limits. Even the grandest valet was not allowed to travel cheek by jowl with his royal master – whether by train or carriage, the valet travelled in a manner befitting his status. He went second class, the lower staff third.

One curious element of the valet's work was described by former valet Eric Horne, whose autobiography, *More Winks*, was published in 1932. Horne described the extraordinary range of items for which he was responsible when his master set off for a weekend in the country. The valet took with him trees for top boots and shoes; brushes for clothes; chamois leathers; a special brush for a hunting coat; dubbing to waterproof boots; oil and line dryers for fishing lines; cartridges and cartridge bags; fishing rods and cases; landing nets; fly boxes and gaffs. Much of the equipment he had to take with him now sounds so unfamiliar as to be incomprehensible – he carried, for example, breeches paste, a boot bone and a hat iron.

But to end on a positive note, many butlers, footmen and valets saw service among royals as infinitely preferable to any other kind of work they might be able to get.

Frank Huggett quotes one footman who described how

we are among beautiful things. Working for the monarch some of the glitter rubs off – we learn good manners; we see and hear polite conversation. It's only in the houses of the middle classes, people not really used to servants, that we are treated like servants – in the royal household a gentleman's servant is treated as a gentleman.

Chapter Four

Animal magic: hunting, shooting and fishing

'I really need a gin and tonic.'
– Queen Camilla after meeting Prince William

'We will never be normal.'
– Harry, Duke of Sussex, to his brother

'If only one's children were more like corgis.'
– Queen Elizabeth II

The royal family has always been more interested in animals than people. Animals can be trusted; humans can't. It's as simple as that – but in a curious paradox that seems to afflict both the royal family and the aristocracy, love of animals is and always has been combined with a love of killing them.

For the English upper classes, animals are split into the loveable – mostly dogs and horses – and the sporting – which means pheasant, grouse and other game birds, deer and, above all, foxes.

The rules of hunting, shooting and stalking have changed over the centuries, but the appeal to the royal family and the upper classes remains the same. Until recently – perhaps around the year 2000 – royal participation in what are known variously as field sports (if you support them) or blood sports (if you don't) was not felt to be particularly controversial, but in more recent times things have changed dramatically.

When surveys suggest that nature and wildlife in the UK is almost in freefall, it seems outrageous to kills stoats and weasels, crows and rooks on the grounds that they eat pheasant chicks and therefore deprive the upper classes and the royal family of their sport.

So, shooting (as well as hunting and stalking) has become a more secretive, guilt-ridden pursuit.

This is a major change from, say, the end of the nineteenth century, when *The Field* magazine was one of the biggest-selling publications in the country; less so perhaps than today, it was then a magazine filled with mindless articles about the vast numbers of pheasants shot by monarchs and their friends at various grand estates up and down the country. In decades past, no one seemed to mind that wildlife was slaughtered unmercifully to ensure that Edward VII in particular but also George V, George VI and even Prince Charles (as he then was) would have plenty of pheasants and grouse to shoot.

Today, with his green credentials to the fore, King Charles likes to emphasise that shooting is good for wildlife in general. This is certainly true in the sense that woodland is essential for pheasant shooting. Landowners don't like keeping woodland if they can't make money out of it, and pheasant shooting is extremely expensive (if you are not a member of the aristocracy) and therefore lucrative. So shooting is a far more carefully conducted business in the twenty-first century, but it is still big business at Windsor and Balmoral, where some shooting days are kept for the royal family and their friends (free of charge) and other days are let to outsiders at exorbitant rates.

Stalking – the shooting of red deer – takes place at Balmoral and is easier to justify: if deer numbers increase unchecked, many of the animals will starve to death in winter, so controlling numbers is a reasonable response. Balmoral, of course, also offers the royals the chance to enjoy some of the world's best salmon fishing, on miles of the river Dee, but as Atlantic salmon continue to decline and are now listed as vulnerable (the result of decades of commercial over-fishing), yet another royal pursuit is coming increasingly under the critical spotlight.

Establishing why the royals are so devoted to hunting, shooting and fishing is difficult. Partly, no doubt, it is just what they do and it is certainly exciting to try to shoot a pheasant rocketing at terrific speed high above woodland. Pheasant shooting is also a sociable business. Guns (meaning those doing the shooting) line out perhaps thirty metres apart, the birds are driven over them and after each drive the guns compare notes and discuss the quality of birds; at lunchtime an elaborate meal is provided (for the royals, this might include silver cutlery and linen napkins brought to the field) and then more drives in the afternoon. Crucially for the royal family, all this can take place well away from prying eyes, and apart from the shooting itself there are other pleasures.

The late Queen Elizabeth II, for example, adored picking up on shoots. 'Picking up' refers to using one's dogs – labradors or spaniels – to find injured birds and despatching (killing) them. Even the best shots injure a lot of birds, which fall to the ground often well behind the guns and into deep cover, where the dogs hunt them out. Elizabeth loved working her dogs in this way – picking up is almost a sport, if that is the right word, in its own right.

Elizabeth's former head keeper at Windsor explained to the present author that the late Queen 'was very good at wringing the injured birds' necks after they had been retrieved by her dogs. One or two of the beaters used to joke that, now and then, she must have wanted to do the same thing to her children!'

The Windsor keeper, who agreed to be interviewed only if he was not identified, was unusually close to the late Queen. She would frequently visit the little bungalow where he lived on the estate after his retirement in the early 1990s and insist on making tea for him and his wife, who knew better than to try to stop her.

In a conversation with the present author, the keeper said:

We worked for her even in retirement. Keepers never really retire and my wife looked after the corgis much of the time because she liked doing it. When I was still working full-time, I ran the shoot at Windsor, so of course I was a servant and would have been treated as such by the Queen's ancestors. But I think she hated the idea that we might see ourselves as servants. She made tea for us every time she visited – she would bustle around the kitchen and say what a relief it was to do something rather than have everything done for her all the time.

On one occasion one of the corgis pestered her for a biscuit and she said to my wife, 'I think he needs a run.' At which she stood up, walked to the door of our bungalow and hurled the biscuit into the garden. The dog shot out after it. She then came back in, sat down and said under her breath, 'If only one's children were so easy to deal with.' In many ways she preferred her dogs and her staff to her family – she liked to say, 'You can choose your staff and your pets, but you can't choose your family.'

The Windsor keeper explained that when he retired, the Queen realised he would need to leave the estate as there was no accommodation available in the grounds of the castle. She immediately asked the estate office to apply for planning permission to build a bungalow for him. Within months the warm, solid little house had been completed.

The keeper said:

I was as amazed as anyone when she offered to build a house for us. We had reconciled ourselves to leaving the estate and then out of the blue we received a message that a house was being built for us. Isn't that extraordinary? You know, she also often paid for the medical bills of her staff if people were sick and could not be seen quickly by the NHS. And when her daughter Princess Anne was almost kidnapped, the Queen paid off the mortgage of the protection officer who helped save her. It's a side of the Queen that is rarely mentioned and little known.

Mind you, when she built our little house, it did mean she could still rely on us to help out a bit – especially with the corgis!

Elizabeth's love of dogs was of course legendary – she owned more than thirty corgis, for example, over her lifetime. As each died, she made sure she had a successor, because her first corgi, Susan, had been a gift from her father, George VI, and always having a corgi was a way to link her to him. All the corgis were descended from that first dog.

Elizabeth II loved corgis and Labradors, but she kept few other breeds. Queen Victoria's love of dogs, by contrast, extended to a range of breeds that long ago dropped out of favour: she had clumber spaniels, Dandie Dinmonts and water spaniels, among others. Her favourite spaniel, Dash, was such a favourite that she insisted he be included whenever her portrait was painted. And as with more recent royals there was always a feeling that Victoria much preferred animals to humans.

Kennelmen traditionally look after the royal dogs, but the corgis have always been given special privileges. Elizabeth II allowed them the run of all her palaces – one footman complained to the present author that half his job involved 'cleaning up after those bloody corgis'. He was instructed to carry a soda siphon and several cloths at all times so that when the corgis peed on the carpets at Buckingham Palace, the offending puddle could be quickly cleaned. 'It was often too far to the nearest exit for the dogs, especially when they got older,' explained the footman. 'And I don't think the royals worried a bit about the state of the carpets – the dogs were always far more important than things. Having so many valuable clocks and paintings all her life meant the Queen took them for granted. She had no interest in them at all!'

Some animals are still kept by the royal family not because they particularly like them, but because they have become part of tradition and keeping them adds a charm to the aura that surrounds the family. Since 1886, the royals have taken part in pigeon racing, a sport embraced by successive monarchs right down to Elizabeth II. So enthusiastic was Queen Victoria's eldest granddaughter Princess Victoria about the birds that she kept a pigeon she refused to travel without. Today, though Charles is apparently so uninterested in the sport that he has declined to take on his mother's patronage of the Royal Pigeon Racing Association, the monarch's racing pigeons remain at the royal pigeon loft at Sandringham, where they are cared for by the Royal Loft Manager.

Other royal pets included George V's African grey parrot, Charlotte. John Wood, who started work below stairs at Sandringham when he was still in his teens, explained to the present author that

George V absolutely loved that bird. He was almost permanently cross with members of his family, but he spoke to that bird as if it was his best friend. It often sat on his shoulder and he didn't mind a bit if it pooped down his suit, which it did all the time. He thought it was hilarious and a small price to pay for what he called his only 'true companion'. We used to joke that it wasn't just his best friend, it was his only friend! He had a small table by his side when he ate dinner and the parrot stayed on this table close enough so the king could feed it with titbits from his own plate.

Though mostly considerate to their shooting staff, the beaters and keepers, the royals could be offhand. John Wood recalled how occasionally a shoot would be arranged, the keepers and assistant keepers would work long hours to get everything ready and then the king and his friends just wouldn't turn up.

I remember once on a very cold morning in early December the keepers waited for hours in the yard and they were too frightened to knock on a door or find someone to ask why nothing was happening. Eventually someone in the household remembered and told them the shooting was cancelled, but by then they'd been waiting outside for more than three hours and it was a day of hard frost. No one complained so far as I can remember. Today [in the early 1980s] the story would have ended up in the newspapers and the Queen would have been embarrassed. Unthinkable back then. We servants thought whatever the king did was above criticism.

Dozens of farm workers and local villagers would also have gathered on that shoot day and then gone home empty-handed. Locals at Sandringham and at Windsor always worked as beaters, trudging through the woods in a long line and tapping sticks to drive the birds forward towards the guns. John Wood recalled, 'They [the beaters] were unpaid but traditionally given a brace of birds each for their efforts. On this particular day, they had to trudge home with nothing to show for three hours in the cold.'

Beating was always the preserve of local people, especially locals who worked on the royal estates as foresters, carpenters and odd job men. If they were asked to beat on a Saturday (shoots were usually on Saturdays and Wednesdays), they could not refuse.

The teams of keepers and beaters also had to make sure that the monarch was in the best position in the line to ensure that more birds flew over him (or her) than over the guests. This was true at the royal estates but also elsewhere when the monarch travelled to visit his friends, as Pamela Horne points out in her 2013 book, *Life Below Stairs*.

Special provision was given to important guests, particularly royalty. That applied at Elveden where George V shot regularly during the 1920s. According to head keeper Tom Turner this affected the shooting plans for the whole season … hand-reared birds would be placed on the beats where his majesty would be asked to shoot and shoots taking place beforehand would not be allowed to encroach on the area required for the royal party … the objective was to secure the largest bag possible and those estates which offered vast numbers of high-flying birds enjoyed a good reputation in game preserving circles. Repeated failure to achieve satisfactory results could lead to a keeper losing his job.

But the big bags at successful shoots can seem almost obscene in the twenty-first century. In his authoritative book *The Great Shoots*, Brian Martin reminds us that in a single day as many as 5,000 birds might be killed by a team of eight or ten guns. That figure might be even higher if royalty happened to be present.

This put huge pressure on keepers to kill everything on an estate that might be thought to compete with or eat pheasants or pheasant chicks. This pressure remains wherever birds are reared for shooting. The law has changed to protect many species from over-zealous keepers, but keepers often flout the law or make mistakes. In 2023, for example, a little owl was caught in a keeper's trap at Sandringham (much to the embarrassment of King Charles), and keepers on the northern moors are occasionally prosecuted for killing rare hen harriers, which eat grouse chicks.

Beaters and keepers were and are servants, their role then as now to provide sport for members of the royal family and their aristocratic friends. It was an exclusive club because you would not be invited to shoot at a great estate unless you yourself owned a great estate and could return the invitation. Buying a day's shooting was seen as dreadfully common.

Aristocrats and royalty did, however, have a slightly nuanced attitude to their shooting servants, especially their keepers; they were seen as a cut above domestic servants and there were as a result curious crossovers. At a shoot visited by the present author in the 1980s, the captain of the beaters was the daughter of an earl. She was also immensely eccentric and to the delight of the twenty or thirty beaters lined out in the woodland at Windsor, she would occasionally shout, 'Will you silly cunts please try to maintain the line.' She never shot or helped out with the pickers-up (both more socially acceptable for a woman of her background) but insisted on being captain of the beaters and even ate lunch with them, sitting with a packet of sandwiches on a log while the royal guns sat at a long linen-covered table nearby.

The captain of the beaters had a vital job ensuring the men (and sometimes women) kept a straight line as they walked through the wood; a crooked line would allow some of the birds to run back through the line, something they would always try to do because pheasants are very reluctant flyers.

The late Queen happened to be picking up at this shoot and she was heard to murmur, 'I don't know if the pheasants are afraid of Lady A, but I certainly am…'

Hunting, by which is meant fox hunting (confusingly, American usage takes 'hunting' to describe what in the UK is known as shooting), has been as much a part of royal life as shooting, and even King Charles has defended the sport despite his enthusiasm for nature and wildlife.

Even today, when in theory only drag hunting is legal, hunts as much as shoots show the old social order in action. The mounted followers are usually aristocrats or local gentry, while the poorer villagers and farm workers follow the hunt by car, on foot or by bicycle. In the past, the style and bravery of the mounted followers was the key thing – being seen on a magnificent horse left the peasants in awe – and the ritual of hunting and being seen to hunt was as much part of the day as the actual pursuit of the fox.

Hunting has become such an emotive and controversial issue

that the royal family no longer keeps its own pack of hounds – with all the hunt servants that would entail – but King Charles was at one time a regular guest of the Duke of Beaufort's hounds. Indeed, Charles's main motivation for buying his country house at Highgrove was its proximity to Badminton, where the Duke of Beaufort's hounds are based.

The social aspect of hunting was traditionally central to its importance. It was at a hunt in Holland that King William III saw the handsome young Arnold Joost van Keppel. When the young man fell from his horse, William was so entranced by his bravery and good looks that he invited him to England and (as we have seen) quickly made him Earl Albemarle, to the jealous fury of former favourites.

Like hunting, shooting often provides introductions for royal men – Prince Charles, as he then was, is said to have first come across Diana Spencer at a pheasant shoot.

The Keppels, aristocratic servants buzzing around the royals like flies ever since Arnold's arrival in England, became very grand indeed and almost overnight. Without hunting, it would not have happened.

In more recent times, horses have been no less important to the royal family. For example, Princess Anne, the second child of the late Elizabeth II, became an Olympic medal-winning horse-woman, a strikingly untraditional sporting achievement made very much in the public eye.

Anne's love affair with horses matched her mother's love affair with dogs; animals could be trusted, unlike ladies in waiting, courtiers and the public. Indeed, Princess Anne once grumbled, 'The horse is the only one who doesn't know I'm royal.'

Her father's view was less complimentary. He insisted, 'If it doesn't fart and eat hay, Anne isn't interested.'

The sport of kings – by which is usually meant horse racing rather than riding – has always been central to royal life. The extent to which this is true can be judged by the fact that a small team of the domestic staff at Buckingham Palace, Balmoral and Sandringham were under strict and permanent instructions to record a list of racing meets on video whenever Queen Elizabeth II was away so that she, and the Queen Mother, could watch them when they returned.

Of course, racing for the royals was only ever a spectator sport, with the added spice – always relished by members of the royal family – of gambling. Dozens of stable lads, trainers and other staff looked after the late Queen's racing stables – she owned more than 100 horses – and her knowledge and enthusiasm meant that over her adult lifetime, her horses won at Ascot a staggering twenty-four times.

Lord Porchester – known to the Queen as Porchey – was the late monarch's racing manager from 1969 onwards, but they had been friends since before the Second World War. Porchester was the epitome of the old-fashioned aristocratic companion serv-ant, a gentleman in waiting in all but name. They met when she was seventeen and he was twenty. It was the start of a lifelong friendship very much in the ancient royal mould.

It is impossible to imagine Elizabeth would have become

equally close to someone further down the social scale. Porchester was the 7th Earl Carnarvon and he was employed not just to advise on the Queen's horses but because, as he put it himself in an interview with TV personality Gyles Brandreth, his father thought he was 'the right sort to accompany Princess Elizabeth to the races'.

That phrase 'the right sort' sums it up. It meant he was sufficiently aristocratic to be a royal companion and adviser.

In addition to his work with the Queen's horses, Porchester became an aristocratic dancing partner for the princess before she became Queen, rather as the Earl of Essex became the dancing partner and friend of Elizabeth I.

Essex was a wonderful dancer and excellent company. But unlike Porchester, Essex overreached himself and lost his head. Even a string of racing failures was always unlikely to lead to a similar fate for Lord Porchester, who died (of natural causes) in 2001.

A former stable lad at Windsor Castle told the present author that every time he saw Porchester with the Queen,

you could see she was madly in love with him. We were convinced that she would have rather married him than Philip, but he wasn't a prince and that made all the difference in those days. The rumour in the servants' quarters was that he was the first handsome man she fell in love with and Philip was the second. She never kissed Porchester in public, but when they met in private, they always greeted each other with a kiss.

Porchester, of course, had all the usual qualifications – an Old

Etonian, he had served in the Royal Horse Guards (inevitably one of the 'best regiments'), so he fitted almost perfectly into the band of acceptable suitors for a second-tier royal, a spare who was unlikely ever to become Queen. That was not the case with Elizabeth, so Porchester became companion, friend and then aristocratic employee. From 1969 until his death, he was Queen Elizabeth's racing manager, an equerry in the original sense of the word, meaning someone who looks after the horses owned by a member of the royal family.

Like so many aristocratic servants down the centuries, Porchester's military background was key. The royals always feel safe with military people, whether in terms of romance or simple employment, and that holds true whether a piper is being employed as an equerry or a special adviser. The appeal of ex-military men is almost as ancient as the royal family itself, which is why even the gillies at Balmoral tend to be men with a military background.

Alec Ogilvie, who was Balmoral head gillie in the 1990s, is a case in point. He served for twenty-two years in the Argyll and Sutherland Highlanders before taking up his role with the royal family, as he explained:

When the royal family arrive at Balmoral each summer, certain regiments always come up to guard them. The Argyll and Sutherland Highlanders was always one of those regiments. While the soldiers are at Balmoral, they also act as beaters, pony men and gillies. In fact, I started my full-time work as a pony man and gillie, having already been on duty here with the regiment.

The royals' love affair with all things Scottish began with Queen Victoria. Earlier monarchs had loathed the idea of the Highlands, which was seen as a uniquely backward and primitive area, until Butcher Cumberland, George II's third and youngest son, largely destroyed the Highland way of life after the Battle of Culloden in 1746.

The Highlands had long been seen as a centre for sedition and Catholic rebellion, but at the end of the eighteenth century and into the early decades of the nineteenth century, this all changed: Scotland was transformed from a 'uniformity of barrenness,' as Samuel Johnson called it in his *Journey to the Western Isles of Scotland*, published in 1775, to a wild, profoundly moving romantic landscape.

Queen Victoria caught the coat tails of this transformation, which affected the Highlands and perhaps even more so the Lake District.

Central to Victoria's idea of the romance of Scotland was the gillie. There is always confusion about what exactly a gillie (or ghillie) is. It's often assumed that a gillie is someone who accompanies and advises salmon anglers and is only involved with fishing. In fact, the word 'gillie' is simply the Gaelic word for a male outdoor servant, which means a gillie can be called upon to help with a range of activities, as Alec Ogilvie explained: 'Depending on the season, gillies at Balmoral help with *all* the sport: they accompany guests to the hill for the deer stalking and to the river for the salmon.'

Alec's father had been a gamekeeper in Stirlingshire, but what tipped the balance in his favour when the gillie's job at Balmoral first came up was probably the fact that he was also an accomplished piper:

> I always played up at the house at the gillies' ball. Two of these were held each year for Queen Elizabeth. The first when the Queen and the rest of the royal family came up in September and the second at the end of October. The gillies' ball is a dance and a dinner and everyone who has helped with or been involved in the grouse shooting, salmon fishing or whatever is invited.

The late Queen always attended the gillies' ball, as a junior gillie recalled:

> She absolutely loved it because she had grown up on it. Dancing was the one time she could completely relax, especially so when she was in Scotland, well away from the newspapers in London. She felt safe among friends and despite being queen she was quite the democrat – remember, it's called the gillies' ball for a reason. The gillies get to take part, which often meant dancing with the Queen herself. She felt safe among these military men who loved fishing and stalking as she did.

Alec Ogilvie was never the only piper at the ball – Queen Elizabeth had her own personal piper who played under her window every morning wherever she was staying, including while she enjoyed her summer at Balmoral.

Queen Elizabeth's personal piper from 2015 to 2019 was Pipe Major Scott Methven. Scott followed the late Queen continually from Balmoral to Buckingham Palace, Windsor to Sandringham and every morning at 9 a.m. in full Highland dress he would play for exactly fifteen minutes under the Queen's bedroom window.

Scott fitted the bill precisely for this sort of appointment. He served two tours of duty in Afghanistan with his regiment before being asked – you don't apply for this sort of job – to take over as the Queen's personal piper. Scott was bemused but insists he loved the job, although he admitted he was rather baffled when told his title included being made a page of the presence. Speaking in 2014, Scott recalled proudly that he had been 'the fifteenth sovereign's piper since 1843'.

But one piper wasn't quite enough, as Alec Ogilvie explained:

The sovereign's own piper is always at the ball, but at least one other piper was always needed, and that was me – the pipers would simply wander round the tables as the guests ate and drank and then play for them when they danced. Always Scottish dancing – and an occasional quick-step.

Many of Alec's memories focus on the late Queen Mother, who always arrived with her party of guests in May:

I gillied for her guests on the hill [stalking] and at the river, but the Queen Mother was an expert and very experienced fisherwoman who knew the river very well under most conditions, so she didn't often need much help. Her guests tended to be friends and ex-employees.

She used to stay for perhaps two or three weeks in May, because that's the best time of the year when most of the fish are caught. Like his grandmother, Charles is also a good fisherman, but then he's been coming here since he was a boy and he knows the river so well.

Gillying is one of the few servant jobs where the boundaries between the boss and the workers are distinctly blurred. Even where royalty is concerned, the gillie is expected to tell the fisherman or woman where to fish and what fly to use.

Another gillie, who did not want to be named, said:

The Queen Mother didn't mind a bit if her gillie told her off for failing to cast in the right place or for retrieving her line too quickly or too slowly. In fact, she would get cross if we were too deferential.

When I was quite junior, we were once wading together in fairly deep water – which is dangerous, you know, although it never bothered the QM. Anyway, I was wading just behind her, offering polite advice now and then and even after she made a few bad casts.

We moved downstream a pace or two and she made a terrible cast. She said, 'I made a complete pig's ear of that, didn't I?'

I had no idea what to say, so I mumbled politely.

She continued to fish and then looked round at me, smiled and said, 'Next time I make a bugger's muddle of a cast, just shout "Christmas" and I will know.'

So that's what I did from then on.

But his favourite story was of the time he was wading with the Queen Mother and she slipped in the fast current.

> I always stood just behind her when she was in deeper, faster water, which was just as well as she lost her footing on one occasion and would assuredly have fallen in if I had not bodily scooped her up. As I righted her, she said, 'You remind me of my husband,' which I took as a great compliment!

He also recalled one of the Queen Mother's more eccentric habits.

> Well, she had a very funny habit whenever she was fishing and nothing was happening – I mean there were no taking fish in the pool we were fishing – she would talk to herself continually. I wanted to know what she was saying, so one day I leaned in and heard again and again the same words, 'Come up, you buggers, come up, you buggers!' She was talking to the fish. She told me later on that the fish 'need encouragement; just like the rest of us'.

The late Princess of Wales grew to dislike Balmoral, although she had grown up in a family where fishing and shooting were as natural as breathing. One of the Balmoral gillies remembered how she liked to tease the more enthusiastic salmon fishers in the family, especially Prince Charles. 'I remember once she was sitting quietly watching all the casting and discussions about which flies to use. She looked a little bored and when everything fell quiet for a moment she called across to Prince Charles, "Darling, wouldn't it be easier to just use a net!"'

Among the more bizarre duties of the gillies was blooding the royal children, a tradition in which a prince or princess's face is smeared with the blood of his or her first kill, whether it happens to be a stag or a fox. King Charles was blooded after his first fox was killed and after shooting his first stag. Charles's daughter-in-law, Catherine, Princess of Wales, has put her foot down and insisted there will be no blooding for her children.

But without servants there would be no field sports for the royals and none of the traditions associated with hunting, shooting and fishing.

There are three 'fishings' at Balmoral: Abergeldie, Balmoral itself and Birkhall, where the Queen Mother used to fish. The total length of river available exclusively to the royals is an extraordinary ten miles. 'And remember,' said one of the gillies, 'the river Dee has some of the best salmon fishing in the world.'

The best fishing at Balmoral is kept exclusively for the royal family, but some is sold. It is very expensive – one week for three or four anglers including accommodation would cost at least £10,000 in 2022 – and it is traditionally expected to be so good in May that to get to fish at this time you might have to wait until someone who has a lease on a particular week dies.

When the fishing ends in September, the gillies' work continues. Alec and all the other gillies would be expected to help with the stalking – a sport that echoes remarkably the passion of earlier monarchs for the chase.

A former pony man at Balmoral explains:

The stalker or gillie – that's the professional, the man employed at Balmoral – takes out the gun, that's what we call the man who will eventually do the shooting. But the stalker knows the hill and he will be aware where the best stags are likely to be. For the royals and their guests, the stalker carries the gun and the ammunition and walks slightly behind the guest gun. We may walk many miles before finding a suitable stag. The stalker then explains to the gun how they will approach the stag – always downwind of the animal and for the last fifty or 100 yards stalker and gillie will be crawling on their bellies through the heather – that's why it's called stalking. You have to stalk the animal. That's where the skill lies. The real skill is not shooting the animal; it's getting into position without the animal sensing you are there, which is very, very, difficult, even for an experienced stalker.

When they are close enough to the animal to get a clean shot, the gillie hands the rifle to the prince, princess or monarch, who then aims at the animal's shoulder or neck and takes the shot. The pony man is always some way behind, but when the stag has been killed, he puts it over the pony's back and the party head back down the hill.

Curiously, the relationship between prince or king and gillie is remarkably unchanged in 600 and more years. In medieval England, the professional huntsman would lead the hunt in pursuit until the stag, exhausted, stood at bay. At that point, the king or prince swung into action, approaching the animal and stabbing it through the heart. Doing this fearlessly and well was key and could make or break a young man's reputation, much as a modern bullfighter is judged on how cleanly he kills the bull with his sword.

King Charles adored stalking as a young man and enjoyed hunting (that is, fox hunting); he was shocked when Diana, who was actually always more comfortable in the city, said she hated shooting, fishing, stalking and hunting – all the main country pursuits so loved by the royals. As a Balmoral gillie put it, 'That, I think, was the start of the deterioration of their relationship, whatever people say about it being entirely about the other woman!'

Chapter Five

Fools, jesters and human pets

'Free your mind and your bottom will follow.'
– SARAH, DUCHESS OF YORK

'When we are born, we cry that we are come
to this great stage of fools.'
– SHAKESPEARE, *KING LEAR*

Royal servants have always been privy to royal secrets. They inevitably hear and see things that seem extraordinary, or endearing, or (occasionally) unpleasant, but there is one group of royal servants who might themselves as a group be described as largely secret. This group has slipped away mostly unnoticed by history for the simple reason that the royal family no longer employs them – but at one time no self-respecting royal court would have been without its dwarves, its jesters and above all its fools.

Royal fools are legendary and yet we know so little about their real everyday lives, despite the fact that they were employed, or more precisely kept, by the royal family for centuries.

And this was not an eccentricity peculiar to the British royal family – for centuries, right across Europe, all royal families kept dwarves and other 'human curiosities' as well as employing fools and jesters.

What is perhaps most extraordinary about this little-known group of royal staff is that they inspired some of the most memorable and intriguing characters in the plays of Shakespeare and his contemporaries.

Indeed, the idea of using humour through the guise of apparent simplicity to criticise, even satirise, the corrupt and overbearing has its origins in the legendary royal fool.

Modern historians argue that royal fools fell into two categories: they were either natural fools (in modern terms they might be neurodiverse, or have learning difficulties of some sort) and artificial fools, individuals who pretended to be simple-minded or foolish in some way but used that cloak of simplicity to say things that no other royal servant could or would dare say. Thus developed the idea, so powerfully present now in literature, that fools were more honest than other men. They were also seen as innocents, which is why their heads are shaved in the few paintings that have come down to us. Shaven heads were also linked to penitence and unworldliness – fools had something of the tonsured nature of monks.

The roles of fool and jester were frequently seen as interchangeable in earlier periods, though there was a growing sense even 400 years ago that jesters were professional entertainers who studied the art of being funny while fools were amusing because of what they were by nature.

In his book *Foole upon Foole*, published in 1605, Robert Armin refers to Henry VIII's Will Somer (*sic*) as the king's 'natural jester' – in other words, he was not acting the fool to entertain; he was instead probably suffering from what we in the twenty-first century might describe as some sort of mental impairment. Fools and jesters were there to entertain, but the fool's jests were typically said to have a bitter edge, an edge that often revealed painful truths.

This idea is most famously embodied in Shakespeare's fool in *King Lear* and there is little doubt that Shakespeare knew well the legends that already by his day surrounded royal fools – Will Sommers, for example, was a household name in Jacobean England despite the fact that he had been dead since 1560. In *King Lear*, the audience's awareness of the fundamental nature of the fool explains why Lear's fool has no name – he is simply the Fool – and there is no doubt that many playgoers at this time would have seen him and other Shakespearean fools as owing a great deal to that legendary figure Will Sommers.

In *Lear*, Shakespeare turns the natural order upside down – the king has become the fool and the fool the wise man. After King Lear gives away his land and power, the Fool continually reminds him of his stupidity. At one point, Lear asks, 'Dost thou call me fool, boy?'

The fool replies, 'All thy other titles thou hast given away...'

And Shakespeare sums up the fool's dilemma, the risks he takes as an honest broker, in 'I marvel what kin thou and thy daughters are: they'll have me whipped for speaking true, thou'lt have me whipped for lying.'

Shakespeare was not the first to conjure the wise fool. Its origins lie further back in history and they are entirely tied up with the idea of monarchy. Despite their low status and acid tongues, fools were always on far more intimate terms with the monarch than any aristocratic adviser. There is something mysterious about this and about the real lives of royal fools – and the mystery allowed powerful legends to grow up around and about fools, legends that saw them as subversive rather than personally powerful, incisive and quick witted rather than physically strong or well connected. They embody perfectly the idea that humour can be a uniquely effective way to show up the pretensions and hypocrisies of the rich and powerful.

It is the fluidity of court life in the early modern period that makes any discussion of fools and other servants difficult. There were no contracts of employment, and anyone could be dismissed in a second without warning; a fool might be dismissed if he ceased to amuse. He might even be handed over to someone else as a gift.

Senior servants might say or do the wrong thing, lower servants might neglect their work, but at least the bulk of royal staff had specific jobs. Royal fools, by contrast, were expected simply to be near or around the monarch, chipping in with sarcastic or otherwise amusing remarks, at the expense, perhaps, of an overbearing courtier; the king would no doubt enjoy seeing a self-important lord teased by someone of no importance at all yet protected by his position close to the monarch. Fools even had their own uniform: rather than the livery worn by most royal servants, they often wore green, a colour associated with innocence and perhaps echoing the idea of simplicity in the Garden of Eden.

To have a fool was not just a prerequisite of kings – Catherine Parr had Jane Foole and Queen Mary kept a dwarf and inherited Will Sommers after her father's death; Elizabeth I had Richard Tarlton.

There has always been an idea that senior servants and courtiers give advice to the monarch while lesser mortals serve the monarch's bodily and practical needs, but the picture in the early modern period is sometimes far more complex than that and this is especially true when it comes to entertainment – and entertainment was a central duty of the royal fool.

Bored with the weight of responsibility, petitioned continually by friends, retainers and staff alike, never quite sure if their nobles would remain loyal, it is no wonder monarchs were desperate for anything that took their minds off the burden of power. If it is true, as Shakespeare has it, that 'uneasy is the head that wears the crown' then it was a large part of the fool's task to ease that uneasy head.

Monarchs had pastimes, it is true – they had hunting, of course, and music and often, in the case of kings, philandering, but laughter must have been a rare and much-valued pleasure. There are many hours to fill when you are king – and so the witty, the entertaining, were always to be found hovering around the court.

But laughter is a dangerous commodity, difficult to control and changing moment by moment from life-enhancing to mocking and cruel, which is perhaps why courtiers often disliked and distrusted their master's fools and jesters, thinking them rough illiterates, coarse, crude and perhaps even irreligious. It is easy to imagine they also disliked someone low-born and ill-educated being so close to the monarch. Fools, jesters, plays and players were not serious, and seriousness was central to the idea of the nobleman's dignity, an idea that lies at the heart of Baldassare Castiglione's famous *Book of the Courtier* (1528), which was widely read, and published in numerous editions in English. This hugely influential guide to succeeding at court insisted that noblemen should always be serious – otherwise how could they possibly expect to be treated seriously?

Few aristocrats before the reign of Charles II wanted to be thought amusing rather than serious, because humour was associated with the lower classes, with clowning and foolishness. We still use the word 'clown' to suggest someone being stupid. Yet in the royal family for centuries, fools and jesters were kept at the heart of courtly life.

Apart from being too frivolous, fools and actors were seen by many as deceivers: playing a part was an act of deception; it was somehow akin to lying, pretending to be something one was not.

The dislike of players and plays explains why in 1642 the theatres were closed; levity was seen as a sure route to sin and hellfire and it had to be stamped out.

But a generation earlier, monarchs had taken a very different view and had even taken part themselves in masques and other revels. Elizabeth I herself commissioned *Twelfth Night* (which included the character Feste, a fool or jester) and Shakespeare is said to have written *The Merry Wives of Windsor* specifically because Elizabeth was so taken with the character of Sir John Falstaff, who had previously appeared in two of Shakespeare's history plays. Sir John is arguably just another kind of fool.

Elizabeth delighted in Sir John no doubt because he reminded her of her own court fool, Richard Tarlton. In his *History of the Worthies of England* (published in 1662), Thomas Fuller writes that 'Tarlton told the Queen more of her faults than her chaplains did'. Elizabeth was famously hot-headed and we know she regularly boxed Tarlton's ears, but she never got rid of him.

Elizabeth I is said to have watched the first performance of Shakespeare's *Twelfth Night* and we know that she adored the character of Sir John Falstaff. Elizabethan and Jacobean players could only function in a world in which they had the support of a nobleman or, better still, the monarch. When Shakespeare's theatre company became 'The King's Men', they became the monarch's servants, protected by but also indebted to the monarch. They became a group of servants on the edge of royal life and the court, ready always to do their master's bidding.

More puritanical monarchs, such as Charles I, may have disliked plays and players, but others have been enthusiasts – an extraordinarily obscene play called *Sodom, or the Quintessence of Debauchery* was probably written for a private performance in front of Charles II by the king's courtier and friend John Wilmot, Earl of Rochester. The play includes a maid of honour called Fuckadilla and an army general called Buggeranthos.

More recent drama enthusiasts have included Queen Victoria,

who adored visiting the theatre as a teenager; many of her draw-ings and watercolours of actors and performances she enjoyed have survived.

For centuries too, members of the royal family even took part in a type of fantasy play that has now vanished: both Henry VIII and Charles I performed in masques, which were courtly entertainments involving music and dancing. They were usually written in such a way as to flatter the reigning monarch, and if the ladies of the court appeared, they were always in elaborate costume and often disguised. Because it was beneath the dignity of royal and noble participants, they did not speak – that was left to professional actors – but they still had the fun of taking part.

Summoning players to court had largely died out by the end of the seventeenth century, but there were exceptions – George IV asked the great comic actor Charles Mathews to perform privately at Carlton House in the early 1830s and Queen Vic-toria asked Charles Dickens to visit her at Windsor Castle and give her a private performance of one of his famous dramatic readings from his own books. He refused repeated invitations through the 1850s and 1860s, finally agreeing to meet in 1870, though he declined to give a reading.

It might be argued that Princess Margaret's invitations to singers and musicians to her parties (parties at which she insisted on singing) were the last gasp of this tradition. In an interview with the present author, a former member of Margaret's staff recalled that

Margaret's parties were always attended by celebrity entertainers

– she liked to invite artistic people, especially musicians and singers. Margaret's mother had been great friends with the playwright and singer Noël Coward among others, so Margaret grew up with a sense that she was part of this world, that, but for being born a princess, she too might have been a professional entertainer. The sad thing is that she always drank too much and seemed rather desperate to show the professionals how talented she was herself and it was all just fuelled by alcohol. I often used to think that her guests were only really there because, well, you can't turn down an invitation from a royal, can you?

* * *

The job of royal fool was taken seriously until well into the eighteenth century right across Europe. A fool, usually though not by any means always male, was as much a servant as any member of the kitchen staff or any aristocratic courtier. And if the monarch kept a fool, so too very often did his or her aristocratic advisers, for in addition to all their complex functions they were also a status symbol. Thomas Cromwell had his fool, as did Sir Thomas More; even the Abbot of Crowland in Lincolnshire kept a fool; and the Pope's Fool Berto was known across Europe.

Peter K. Andersson's detailed and carefully researched book *Fool* explains how complex and multifaceted the idea of the royal fool became. They were, he says, a reminder to the elevated that lesser mortals exist in the real world. Echoing the wise or holy fool vaguely sanctioned by scripture, they not only made jokes but also acted as the butt of other people's cruel jokes; they were mocked but they also allowed the most fortunate to enjoy the pleasure of pitying the least fortunate.

Fools at court were also in a unique position vis-à-vis the monarch. It was impossible to imagine they might be a threat, unlike many aristocratic courtiers, who were often closely related by blood to the monarch and might one day foment a rebellion in an attempt to take the crown by force. But fools were also seen as too simple to fake their real feelings, which means there was an idea that when they spoke, they spoke only the truth – in contrast to courtiers, who only ever said what would impress the monarch or what would at least not arouse the monarch's anger. Courtiers were too polite, too self-interested to tell the truth often – it was simply too dangerous – but fools could do it, or at least that was the popular perception.

Fools might therefore become surprisingly close to their masters, which may explain why in several portraits of Henry VIII, William Sommers can be seen in the background. The key fact here is that in these portraits only family members appear – family members and royal fools. The implication is that the fool was seen as a family member rather than strictly a member of staff. Henry clearly saw Sommers as one of the family, but a subservient member. There is evidence that he was occasionally beaten for his bluntness. But he was beaten in the way a favourite dog might be beaten. If that suggests Sommers was seen more as a kind of intelligent pet, we are much closer to the truth than we might imagine – Robert Armin, for example, suggests Sommers slept with the king's spaniels.

Will Sommers became the archetype of the royal fool. He is

mentioned in numerous books published after his death, and large numbers of jokes and anecdotes were attributed to him. Many have little real, provable connection to him at all, but the fact that they seemed to fit the Sommers legend tells us a great deal about what he was perceived to be and his importance as a symbol outside courtly circles.

Some of the stories attributed to Will Sommers are fairly crude examples of humour – he throws a pudding at a rival fool, for example, or is himself kicked down a flight of stairs for his cheek, but others speak of real mental agility: in a story from Thomas Wilson's *The Arte of Rhetorique* published in 1553 and quoted by Robert Andersson, Henry VIII needed to call in money that was due to him. During a conversation between Henry and his advisers, a conversation that took place in front of Sommers, reference was made to the money coming from 'Auditours, Receivers and Survueighours [surveyors]'.

Sommers immediately piped up and told the king that the problem was that he had 'so many Frauditours, and so many Conueighers [counterfeitors] and Deceiuers … that they get all to themselves'. It's a brilliant commentary posing as malapropism.

The fool as holy innocent, subtle though simple adviser and humorous pet – these were the more positive sides of the role of the royal fool, but there was a darker side.

The desire to have someone at court who had what we would see today as mental health issues or learning difficulties is a precursor to the sort of 'entertainment' we see Londoners enjoying in the eighteenth century when they visited the Bedlam mental hospital to laugh at the inmates' antics. Sommers and other royal fools were kept in part at least so the monarch and his or her friends would have someone to laugh *at* as well as to laugh *with*. Visiting the 'fools and lunatics' at Bedlam showed you were sane and middle class; owning your own fool showed you were sane and upper class or royal.

The desire to own what the royal family and the nobility thought of as collectable 'human curiosities' lasted well into the modern era. As late as 1720, George I kept a young man at Kensington Palace who was only ever known as Peter the Wild Boy. Peter had apparently been found naked and running about on all fours in a remote woodland area in Germany while George was hunting. The boy appeared to have survived alone in the woods, living, presumably, on nuts and berries. He was found aged around twelve and brought to London, where he lived at Kensington Palace long enough to be included in a painting on the walls of the great staircase that can still be seen today. Peter – who is now thought to have been suffering from Pitt–Hopkins syndrome, a condition that causes developmental delay and often epilepsy – fascinated and entertained London society for a few years, but then his curiosity value faded and he was sent to live for the rest of his long life – he died in 1785 – on a farm in Hertfordshire. Peter's appeal was that he seemed the living embodiment of untutored innocence, a creature from before the fall of man, natural and untamed, an amusing innocent.

The story of the so-called Wild Boy found originally in a forest (or so the legend goes) is neatly summed up by William Henry Pyne in his *History of Royal Residences* published in 1819:

He was sent over to England in April 1726 and ... brought before his majesty and the nobility. He could not speak and scarce had any idea of things but was pleased with the ticking of a watch, the splendid dresses of the king and princess and endeavoured to put on his own hand a glove that was given to him by her royal highness.

He was dressed in gaudy habiliments but at first disliked this confinement and much difficulty was found in making him lie on a bed; he, however, soon walked upright and often sat for his picture. He was at first entrusted to the care of the philosophical Dr Arbuthnot who had him baptised Peter; but notwithstanding all the doctor's pains, he was unable to bring him to the use of speech or to the pronunciation of words ... he resisted all instruction and existed as a person allowed in succession by the three sovereigns in whose reigns he lived. He resided latterly at a farm near Berkhamsted in Hertfordshire until February 1785 where he died at the supposed age of nearly ninety.

We have to remember that no one viewed mental impairment as a purely medical issue at this time; such a view would have been impossible in an era when mental problems were still seen as having as much to do with demons, devils, fairies and monsters as with what then passed for medical science.

But for all their entertainment value, their occasional insights and charm, royal fools however brilliant could not ultimately match the status bestowed by birth; the idea of the artistic genius being superior to the aristocrat who enjoys his status simply by virtue of his birth was still a long way off.

Sommers, like Queen's Mary's court innocent, Jane Foole (who also appears in at least one portrait of the royal family), was still a servant. His role was to provide companionship; to be a friendly, amusing presence among so many schemers. It was assumed he would not scheme, and for a king surrounded by pretend friends it must have been a comfort to have Sommers around. The idea that he might leave the king's service was unthinkable. He could only leave if he was dismissed and the same was always true for other servants across the social scale. Why on earth would anyone leave and risk the monarch's displeasure?

Keeping human curiosities was linked to another fashion that spread across Renaissance Europe. Rich men collected oddities of nature – narwhal horns, animal teeth, skulls, minerals, African masks, feathers from rare birds – and kept them in so-called cabinets of curiosities. Their popularity coincided with the opening up of the world by explorers, and royalty and the aristocracy became avid collectors. Fools and even more so dwarves and other human curiosities such as Peter the Wild Boy became part of these cabinets of curiosities.

Owning a sophisticated human pet would not have been seen in any way as inappropriate or morally questionable at this time, which is why among other royal servants there were also court dwarves.

Jeffrey Hudson, born in 1619, probably suffered from some kind of growth hormone deficiency, but whatever the cause he never grew to above two feet in height. While still a child, he was given to the Duchess of Buckingham. We do not know if his family was forced to hand the child over, but they probably thought their son would have a better life in an aristocratic household. This was complicated by the fact that Jeffrey's father worked for the Duke of Buckingham as a bull keeper, a lowly job that involved raising fighting bulls that were transported south of the river Thames to be pitted against dogs.

The Duchess of Buckingham later decided that Jeffrey, the star attraction in her cabinet of curiosities, would make a suitable gift for Charles I's Queen Henrietta Maria. At a spectacular dinner, Jeffrey was wheeled into the banqueting hall hidden in a large pie, from which he then emerged, no doubt to the great delight of the Queen, whose property he then became.

Dwarves, fools and, increasingly, black servants were not usually mistreated because they were highly valued as status symbols, and they were often paid with money or clothing.

The earliest record we have of a black servant comes from the first decade of the sixteenth century, when court documents show a black trumpeter, one John Blanke, was paid eight pence a day by Henry VII.

Perhaps at the deepest level the royal family kept dwarves, fools and black servants because human curiosities were expensive, very expensive; they were yet one more way for the royal family to show that they were above everyone else. They could collect not just curiosities from the natural world but also human beings.

It might be thought that in the twentieth and twenty-first centuries there are no fools left in royal service. One former member of the below-stairs royal staff insists that the opposite is true if you are happy to include 'oddballs, misfits and eccentrics'.

Royal service at the top end often attracts the more eccentric kind of aristocrat – it always has. In fact, many of those with more practical jobs in the palace like me [former junior footman] thought many of the old-fashioned and very grand courtiers were so eccentric as to be a waste of space. They seemed to sort of pop up now and then but doing very little, but they looked and sounded right – you know, the right kind of accent and background. I suspect many were distant relatives [of the royals]. And there was definitely an overlap between family members who were always on the fringes of the royals but were unimportant themselves. People like the late Lord Lichfield, who was almost permanently drunk and often embarrassing, but like a medieval courtier he would never be removed just for being drunk and useless. In the words of Queen Elizabeth II, he was 'one of us', so he was always welcome.

Other former members of staff recall the antics of what one called 'the dotty old nobs brigade'.

Judy Morris's mother Edith was in royal service just after the end of the Great War. Judy recalled her mother saying,

We really did think that many of the well-born courtiers were completely mad. They could not have been employed in proper jobs outside the palace because they were so eccentric and impractical, but the senior royals liked having them around. They were entertaining more than anything and perhaps reassuring that the old order was still important, but they could do the most bizarre things.

Judy went on herself to work for the royals at Buckingham Palace in the 1950s. She recalled:

I had to clean the office of one elderly courtier and I remember hating to go in if he was there. He was always muttering odd things under his breath. One phrase he continually muttered to no one in particular and in a very high-pitched voice was 'Happy little team', followed by 'Cha-cha-cha-cha'. Sometimes I would see him lowering things out of his window on a piece of string and at Sandringham he apparently used a large megaphone to shout at the gardening staff through his bedroom window.

Then there was the courtier who remained absolutely silent but every now and if he saw someone he hadn't seen for a while or needed to express surprise he would say, 'Funk and Wagner!' Or 'Tell that to the marines'. We never had a clue what he was talking about or why he said these things, but he was always around and we simply assumed he was a distant relative [of the royal family] who had nothing to do and so was given a job, if you can call it a job, as a courtier.

The truth is that until relatively recently the royal family kept on many of their aristocratic advisers precisely *because* they were slightly nutty – they were entertaining, just like medieval jesters!

Chapter Six

Friends in very high places

'Everywhere you looked you were tripping over bloody Keppels.'
– WILLIAM TALLON, AKA BACKSTAIRS BILLY,
ON LIFE IN ROYAL SERVICE

*'Amongst us, the badge of gentry is idleness: to be of no calling,
not to labour, for that's derogatory to their birth...'*
– ROBERT BURTON, *THE ANATOMY OF MELANCHOLY*

*'There is no labour comparable to the labours of a prince.
These labours are greater than all the labours of the body.'*
– BISHOP JOHN JEWEL, QUOTED BY KEITH THOMAS
IN *THE ENDS OF LIFE*

It may be obvious, but it is also profound: there is no point being a king if you are not surrounded by people who behave towards you as one behaves towards a king. Kings are only kingly in the glow of deference, in the light shone by those who surround them. This is why in the early modern period, and to some extent still today, monarchs are very much public property. When the late Queen Elizabeth II said, 'We have to be seen to be believed,' she meant that monarchs cannot be believed in and supported if they are not always in the public eye.

During Charles II's reign, pretty much anyone could join him for his daily walk surrounded by courtiers and spaniels as he crossed Whitehall towards to St James's Park. It was assumed that no one would even think of attacking God's anointed and therefore security was unnecessary, although of course if you were not dressed as a gentleman, you were likely to be kicked and cuffed by a member of the nobility if you ventured too close to the monarch.

When a monarch dined, it was also a semi-public affair surrounded by ceremony and although monarchs and their families are no longer watched by courtiers and the nobility, eating is still seen as something a monarch will do on behalf of the government when there are visiting heads of state. A banquet is almost always the highlight of a state visit and no modern monarch would be able to refuse to host such an event.

Even when monarchs had genuine political power before the so-called Glorious Revolution of 1688, they would be wary of refusing to see their ministers and nobles. Edward II was dethroned and eventually killed because as well as probably being gay he mixed with carpenters and thatchers, stonemasons and boatmen instead of the nobility. Today, a monarch with the common touch would be applauded; in earlier times, it might cost you your life.

So, a king is a king only if he takes his rightful place at the high table.

As Alison Sim puts it in *Masters and Servants in Tudor England*, the court, like a nobleman's house, was meant to be a community and that community was head of numerous other communities down the chain of being: the husband rules his wife; the husband is ruled by his lord; the lord rules the local area, the king rules all the lords and by extension therefore the whole country (an extended community) and the Pope is the head of the world community of Christians. God was head of everything. It was dangerous to disrupt the natural order, the chain of being, as King Lear discovers when he gives away his kingdom in Shakespeare's play.

To be royal is to be surrounded by large numbers of people whose daily lives as servants and aides and companions bear witness to the importance of the person at the centre of a great hive of activity. A king living in isolation in a remote castle would be vulnerable to losing his crown, but he would also hardly be considered a king at all.

So, staff conferred status, which is why England's royal courts have always been home to huge numbers of servants. Just take the religious servants of the crown in the Tudor period, for example. As Alison Weir points out, the chapels royal alone employed at least ten clerks, plus the dean of the chapel; the children of the chapel (the choir); the yeoman of the vestry, who looked after the vestments, candles and other essentials; and the clerk of the closet, who prepared the chapel each day.

Servants, followers, advisers and courtiers – in their sheer numbers they reflected power, wealth and patronage, which is why their numbers have tended to increase out of all proportion to the numbers actually needed to do the job. It was more dignified to have three or four servants doing one job even if that job was completely unnecessary. And monarchs have always hated cutting back, since cutting back is perceived as a loss of prestige. This is why Queen Victoria refused to get rid of her falcon keeper – who was paid £1,400 a year (an enormous sum in mid-Victorian England) – even though she owned not a single falcon.

The life to which the English aristocracy has always aspired mirrors that of the monarch. To be a monarch or a member of the aristocracy was and to some extent still is defined by how many people you can afford to pay to ensure you yourself are able to remain completely idle.

But at court, prestige was a two-way affair. If having many servants bolstered the monarch's sense of his or her importance, so too working for the royal family bolstered many people's sense of *their* own importance.

The royal household had originally been composed of the king, his family, his retainers and the senior members of the nobility who were able to raise armies for the king if necessary. Very few women other than a queen's personal attendants were employed in the medieval court. The senior members of the king's or queen's entourage in turn had servants who lived at court and they would try to get their sons as well as their friends and relatives into court positions. Even a fairly lowly servant might himself have at least one servant. Married male servants often had to house their wives away from the court, visiting them only occasionally. Aristocratic retainers might see their wives only a few times each year. As a rule, keeping the nobility close was essential if a king's position were to remain secure.

Aristocrats in turn knew that they must always be close to the monarch if they were to progress in the only world they knew or cared about. A useful piece of advice or an amusing comment while in the king's entourage might mean a valuable sinecure or an additional title or a gift of large tracts of land. Sometimes these gifts were so extravagant or out of proportion to the merits of the recipient that they were blocked by Parliament. In 1700, for example, William III gave his young favourite Arnold Joost van Keppel thousands of acres in Ireland, but Parliament was so outraged – apart from being young and charming, Keppel had done nothing to deserve such a gift – the king was forced to change his mind.

And if courtiers and other servants followed the king to bed and to dinner, they also followed when a monarch visited his various palaces around the country or indeed when he visited the houses of his aristocratic subjects. Legend has it that Elizabeth I's regular progresses around the country bankrupted many smaller landowners, who had to entertain the queen in addition to as many as 100 of her servants and attendants. According to Alison Sim, even a visit to chapel on Sunday would involve a huge procession of officials and attendants and staff – every noble on hand, including foreign visitors, would be expected to attend.

Some traditions are identical today – when a monarch died in the early modern period, chief officers of the household would break their rods of office over the grave, and exactly the same ceremony was performed by the Lord Chamberlain at Elizabeth II's burial in 2022.

In many ways this most recent royal funeral was less democratic than that of Elizabeth I 400 years earlier: when Elizabeth I died, the whole household, from the cleaners and kitchen boys through the women of the bedchamber to attendant lords, walked behind her coffin. No kitchen staff were invited to follow Elizabeth II's coffin. Even – perhaps especially – in death, community was everything.

And community, the bonds of service and family, meant that almost every servant's post at court depended not on what one knew but on who one knew.

Rather than seeing this as nepotism, a practice that in the west at least would be seen today as somewhat corrupt, it was seen in the early modern period as the glue that kept the court and for that matter society together. Networks of relationship and obligation were powerful. The monarch might offer lucrative posts to his aristocratic courtiers, but down in the kitchens the cook would exercise similar patronage by offering more junior jobs to friends and relatives.

Men sensed when a particular courtier's star was in the ascendant and he would be petitioned and befriended by all those who could muster a reason for being near him. But a man in disgrace would be abandoned just as quickly, since association with a courtier in disfavour would almost certainly damage those closest to him. In extreme cases where a courtier was accused of treason, it might even lead to the death of his associates.

Shakespeare sums this up neatly in these lines from *King Lear*, spoken by the Fool: 'Let go thy hold when a great wheel runs downhill lest it break thy neck with following, but the great one that goes uphill, let him draw thee after.'

The power of the most aristocratic of all servants to patronise their friends can perhaps best be seen in the career of Elizabeth I's closest and most trusted adviser, William Cecil. She called him her 'spirit' and whatever else he was, he was certainly good at spiriting away goods and gifts.

Cecil had a large number of crown offices in his gift. As a trusted senior servant, he had himself been given a highly lucrative job as Master of the Wards, a sinecure that allowed him to do as he pleased with the income from estates that had been inherited by wealthy children. Each child represented one wardship. Cecil was already immensely wealthy, so he gave at least thirty wardships to his friends and servants, who in turn used them to enrich themselves.

Helping yourself to money in the royal purse could be dangerous, but not if you were a favourite of the monarch. When the Duchess of Marlborough helped herself to several thousand pounds from Queen Anne's Treasury in the early 1700s, nothing was done because she was the queen's closest confidante.

So deeply embedded was the idea that it was perfectly natural to use one's friends and relatives to one's own advantage that corruption was endemic. Just as corruption among aristocratic aides and servants was tolerated, so too was a different kind of corruption much lower down the social scale. Kitchen staff expected to supplement their incomes by stealing food and candles; they invited their friends and relatives to eat with them; they often split their own jobs in order that a friend or family member should get a place. Everyone in the royal household was open to bribes or gifts, which were given with the expectation that they would be reciprocated.

Keith Thomas in *The Ends of Life* neatly summarises the situation: 'Throughout the early modern period advancement in most walks of life depended primarily on family and friends, patronage and connection. This was the case in government and public office, in the church, in business and in the professions.' And, one might add, at court.

Today, of course, peerages are often bestowed much as wardships and sinecures were given in the sixteenth and seventeenth centuries. In the past, a favourite of the monarch might find himself a knight one day and a lord the next; today, things are not that different, with peerages frequently given to friends of those in power.

In the past, royal gift giving at the highest level could include arranging advantageous marriages. In 1517, for example, Cardinal Wolsey told a friend that he would arrange for him to marry an exceptionally wealthy widow. While Wolsey was manoeuvring to make this happen, a close friend of the king, Nicholas Carew, persuaded Henry to insist the widow should marry one of Carew's friends. Even the great Wolsey knew when he was beaten, but he was furious. The widow, of course, had little say about the marriage.

The idea of women as symbols of status and wealth trickled down from the royal family through the aristocracy to the middle classes, and from medieval times through to the twentieth century. A servant interviewed by the present author recalls a row between her employer and his wife in the 1960s. The husband insisted that his wife must not work in case his friends thought he was unable, financially, to keep her; he also insisted that he would be disgraced if she did not employ staff to look after her children and do the housework rather than look after them herself.

The system of patronage among servants and courtiers has had other lasting consequences down to the present: many of Britain's wealthiest aristocratic lineages – the Throckmorton, Carew, Knatchbull, Percy, Howard and Knollys families – enjoy their wealth and position today because their ancestors were royal servant companions. In many cases, these families – still the main source of courtiers – are also blood relatives of the royal family. The late Diana Spencer was a distant cousin of her husband, Prince (now King) Charles, for example, and if Lord Mountbatten, King Charles's uncle, had had his way, Charles would have married another distant cousin, Amanda Knatchbull.

These relationships that began centuries ago with patronage, gifts and sinecures for royal favourites continue to this day. Today's aristocratic royal servants are often directly descended from long-dead aristocratic servants. Sir Derek Keppel was an aristocratic courtier for decades. In his long career, he worked for George V, Edward VIII and George VI. He was the son of Lord Albemarle, a direct descendant of Wiliam III's favourite

Arnold Joost van Keppel, and the brother of George Keppel who married Edward VII's favourite mistress, Alice Keppel.

The world of the courtier was and to some extent still is incredibly incestuous.

Despite his aristocratic status, Sir Derek had rather mundane tasks to perform: the historian Adrian Tinniswood notes that 'he was in charge of 120 clerks, secretaries and manservants and another eighty female cleaners and maids'.

As we have seen, having large numbers of servants – whether aristocratic aides or domestic staff – is still necessary to maintain the almost magical idea that the royal family must be seen to be living, almost, in another century. Indeed, royal status through servant numbers perhaps reached its apogee in the nineteenth century. As Adrian Tinniswood puts it, 'Did [Queen Victoria] really need thirty-three medical men?'

But all monarchs struggle with these things. Growing up surrounded by deference, royal princes and princesses believe instinctively in their right to live at a certain level. What seems immensely extravagant to an ordinary person can seem a minimum level of staff for a royal. King Charles no doubt thinks it is perfectly reasonable, given his status as king, to have a member of staff tasked with putting toothpaste on the royal toothbrush each evening.

Like most monarchs, King Charles simply cannot do without a certain number of servants. In 2022, the annual cost of his staff was £23.7 million; a year later, it had risen to £26.9 million – and that is the bill only for the salaries paid from the sovereign grant (i.e. from the money King Charles receives from the taxpayer).

It does not include the dozens of people employed at Charles's numerous mansions and at Queen Camilla's home in Wiltshire.

Of course, many of today's royal servants may only rarely see King Charles or Queen Camilla. Beds are made and apartments cleaned discreetly, at times when the royals themselves are absent. But the picture is rather different with some staff.

Take equerries, for example. The word 'equerry' originally meant a servant who looked after the royal horses, but like so many royal servant titles, the equerry's job has changed out of all recognition over the centuries. Rather than working in the stables, equerries now advise and provide companionship for the monarch, and a king may have as many or as few as he chooses. King Charles III has twelve equerries; almost all are from the upper classes, and they usually have a military background. Choosing military men has no rational basis beyond the certainty that there is no risk with an officer from one of the 'best' regiments that Charles will be saddled with a lower-class equerry. Certain regiments have always had a connection with royalty, and officers from those regiments can be assumed to include only the 'right sort'. In truth, monarchs choose their senior staff and closest advisers today in much the same way their ancestors did half a millennium ago.

The traditional equerry has survived many scandals. One of Edward VII's equerries, Lord Somerset, was allowed to leave the country after being caught in a gay brothel, for example. Nor were equerries always guaranteed to kowtow to their masters. In *Behind the Throne*, Adrian Tinniswood recounts the story of Fritz Ponsonby, equerry to both Edward VII and George V. Ponsonby was challenged to a game of tennis by George – whether or not George felt Ponsonby should have let him win is not recorded, but we know that having been soundly beaten by Ponsonby, George went into a huge sulk. When George challenged another of his equerries, George Keppel, to a game, hoping he might do better, he was once again beaten and descended into yet another sulk. Aristocratic servants, unlike domestic servants, were clearly getting a little above themselves.

Many equerries thought of themselves as very little lower on the social scale than their royal masters and they expected royal service to keep them in the style they felt was their due. According to Adrian Tinniswood, Bryan Godfrey-Faussett, another of George V's equerries, continually complained to the king about his poverty despite employing ten servants at home.

Fritz Ponsonby was unusual in that not only did he refuse to flatter the king; he also hated those who did flatter him. Other equerries became very close to the monarchs for whom they worked. Arthur Bigge, Baron Stamfordham, was George V's private secretary, and the king once wrote to him, 'I thank God I have a friend like you.' Like a number of British monarchs, George V preferred his staff to his own children. In fact, according to a number of biographers and even George V's own librarian, Owen Morshead, he was a terrible father who beat his sons and reduced his second son, later George VI, to a timid, stammering wreck.

Kings and queens have never worried about shouting at or otherwise abusing their children, their equerries or their other staff, but few have gone so far as Elizabeth I, who, in a rage with her chamberer Mary Scudamore, beat her so badly that one of Mary's fingers was broken. And even that great friend of monarchy Arthur Bigge, for whom George V thanked God, occasionally came in for abuse. George frequently bellowed at him. In an interview with the present author, Agnes Cooke, who worked in the royal kitchens for many years, recalled that George had 'the foulest temper [and used] the foulest language any of us had ever heard. He would occasionally shout "cunt" or "just fuck off" at his personal staff for no reason at all except his bad temper.'

Agnes Cooke thought one of George's problems was that he did not have enough to do and he was constantly in the company of equerries and other upper-class staff who also didn't have much to do beyond keeping the king amused.

In this bored, hot-house atmosphere, it is perhaps no wonder the king frequently lost his temper. Quirks and eccentricities that might seem amusing at one time might just as quickly become irritating – in both a king and his staff – and certainly George was eccentric. At Christmas one year, for example, his gift to the very young children of one of his equerries was an ashtray each.

And equerries have never come cheap. They are paid, like all gentlemen servants, at a rate that reflects not what they do but their social position.

In 2024, the satirical magazine *Private Eye* reported that it was costing the Ministry of Defence almost half a million pounds a year to provide equerries to work for the royal family; the young men taking turns were all from the traditional aristocratic regiments.

Of course, the danger of having friends in very high places is that sometimes those friends start to believe they are rather more important than they really are. It was one thing to visit a male brothel or complain to the monarch about poverty but quite another to try to marry the monarch's sister, as Peter Townsend did when he famously wooed Princess Margaret. Townsend might have got away with it if he had been an aristocrat, but he was decidedly middle class and that really was beyond the pale.

Having friends in high places can lead to enormous embarrassment on both sides – friends of the royals who become unofficial (or official) advisers can live to regret their connection and the royals themselves occasionally regret becoming too close to their advisers.

Perhaps the most embarrassing adviser–royal relationship was that between Prince Charles, as he then was, and TV personality and paedophile Jimmy Savile.

Earl Mountbatten of Burma, Charles favourite uncle, had taken a shine to Savile as early as 1966. So much so that Savile became the first civilian to be awarded a green beret, making him an honorary Royal Marine. When Savile died, he was buried with his green beret. Mountbatten introduced Savile to Charles, who quickly took to him, and Savile became Charles's media adviser, marriage guidance counsellor and party planner. He was even considered as a godfather for William and Harry and at one point Charles felt Savile should join his staff on a formal basis. Luckily for Charles, Savile preferred the limelight of television.

Like many royals, King Charles has no real experience of the world outside the strange atmosphere of royal deference; as a result, he is perhaps both over-confident and insecure, which is why his advisers tend to come and go. Enthusiasm for a particular media adviser's abilities is often followed quickly by disillusionment, but the enthusiasm for Savile lasted until and beyond Savile's death in 2011. On Savile's eightieth birthday, Charles sent him a box of cigars and a letter which said, 'Nobody will ever know what you have done for this country, Jimmy.'

Chapter Seven

A real revolution

'Only the mad girls chase me.'
– William, Prince of Wales

*'I read that 80 per cent of British men would
rather sleep with a goat than me.'*
– Sarah, Duchess of York

It's the scale of the thing that astonishes: by the 1860s, more than forty housemaids were employed at Windsor Castle; forty more were employed at Buckingham Palace.

In 2024, more than 800 staff were employed at Buckingham Palace. The vast building contains ninety-two offices and 188 staff bedrooms. Vast teams of domestic staff are matched by vast teams of communications and administrative staff, and they are not especially well paid given the wealth of the royal family. In 2012, for example, the average annual salary of Prince Charles's (now King Charles's) staff was £33,000.

Some of the staff have what many would consider ridiculous

jobs: as Prince of Wales, Charles insisted that one member of his staff should always accompany his master, carrying with him a loo seat covered in white leather, a curious modern echo of the close stool carried centuries earlier by the Groom of the Stool.

Other curious jobs that continue to this day include the full-time clock winders and repairers, the flag serjeants and the fender-smiths – but then the royal family has always had lots of clocks and watches to wind.

Queen Victoria always carried a timepiece, but she expected it to be wound each morning by a specially trained servant; her son's favourite mistress, Alice Keppel, complained to a friend that her maids were too stupid to be relied on to always remember to wind the half-dozen watches she owned (several of them being gifts from Edward).

One step further were those aristocrats who thought even owning a watch was beneath them – Queen Victoria's favourite minister, Lord Melbourne, hated carrying a watch, so he employed someone to accompany him and tell him the time when he needed to know.

Nancy Jackman, interviewed by the present author in the 1980s, worked for the royal family in the 1920s and remembered her friend Daisy's account of life in the royal family's retreat at Sandringham and the oddities of the king's attitude to time:

Daisy told me George V insisted when at Sandringham that all the clocks should be set half an hour fast so that he would never be late for his shooting. He also insisted that the clock in the servants' hall should have its bell removed because he claimed it disturbed him. It was an old grandfather clock and it was loud but I'm sure the king couldn't hear it at all or only faintly, but he was very bad-tempered and took against things for no reason. He also disliked us servants even though he had dozens. The only person he liked was his gamekeeper! And I include his wife in that general dislike – he treated her as if she was a dog or a slave. But without the bell in the clock the staff got in a terrible muddle because we all relied on hearing it strike the hours to know when it was time for various things we had to do. When we were late, no one blamed the king for silencing the clock; they blamed us! I can tell you, George V was almost completely mad – if he was horrible to his wife, he was worse to his sons. Called them all sorts of terrible things, hit them, told them they disgusted him. He didn't care if the servants heard the abuse because I really think he thought we were pieces of furniture who couldn't hear anything! But he saved most of his rage for the various clocks around the house. He used to growl at them and mutter curses under his breath and the growling and cursing were very similar to the way he growled and cursed at the servants. I think he thought clocks and servants were one and the same thing and all out to get him! And he had huge numbers of both!

But if, as we have seen, the number of servants employed expanded to fit the status (and finances) of the royal family, there was a historical precedent for this. In his *Time Traveller's Guide to the Middle Ages*, Ian Mortimer describes the extraordinary numbers of attendants and servants employed by the royal family in the early modern period: 'Edward II has 450–500 men in his household in 1318. Edward III has considerably more than 800 in the period 1344–70 ... in the more peaceful 1360s he has between 350–450.' Among these there were 'eight chamber knights, twenty-five clerks, three serjeants at arms, one hundred and one esquires, eighty-nine valets of the stables and fifty-three grooms'. There were just two cleaners.

The number of royal servants had not significantly decreased half a millennium later. Queen Victoria constantly pushed to have more servants – reducing staff numbers was not in keeping with her sense of her own dignity, so at any one time she employed around 300 servants.

That said, some of the richest landowners in the country could match this and Victoria was impressed by wealth and servant numbers. The Grosvenor family, now the richest family in the UK (not excepting the royals), were ennobled by Victoria solely because she couldn't bear the idea that such a wealthy family should not have a title that matched their enormous wealth.

She was always conscious of the wealth of others; when she visited the Marquess of Stafford at his home Stafford House (now Lancaster House) a short distance from Buckingham Palace, she said to him, 'I come from my house to your palace.' The marquess, later the 1st Duke of Sutherland, employed enough servants to make even Victoria envious.

The difficulty with having enormous numbers of servants was that a way had to be found to keep them in order and keep them working hard and behaving in a manner acceptable to their employers.

Nancy Jackman recalled what happened when her great-aunt decided to leave her job as a maid at Buckingham Palace.

As soon as she said she wanted to leave, the senior below-stairs staff were outraged. It was as if she had insulted them by wanting to go, but she was lucky. They gave her a reasonable reference, where in many instances people who left the royal family's employment were given either no reference or a reference that meant that would never again get a job with a decent family. It was a system designed to control servants and keep them in their place.

Wider society joined in this battle to make sure domestic staff knew and stayed in their place. The *Servants' Magazine*, which was published for many years during the nineteenth century, emphasised that servants should never question their masters, that they should always do exactly what they were told to do and, perhaps most telling, that they should always be subservient. It was not their place to question their betters, so said an editorial. This idea of subservience ran deep and as late as 1870 the *Englishwoman's Domestic Magazine* published an article on how best to whip young female domestic servants.

Before the Great War, servants whether royal or otherwise would be given the sort of advice contained in *A Few Rules for the Manners of Servants*, published by the Ladies' Sanitary Association in 1893 and quoted in Pamela Horn's *Life Below Stairs in the Twentieth Century*. The book's advice to servants consists largely in explaining an endless list of things they must *not* do. The implication of many of the rules seems to be that any physical contact between servant and master might lead to contamination:

> Do not walk in the garden unless permitted or unless you know that all the family are out, and be careful to walk quietly when there, and on no account to be noisy.
>
> Never sing or whistle at your work where the family would be likely to hear you. When meeting any ladies or gentlemen about the house, stand back or move aside for them to pass.
>
> When you have to carry letters or small parcels to the family or visitors, do so upon a small salver or hand-tray.
>
> If obliged to take anything in the hand, or to lift it off the salver, do not give it to the person to whom it belongs, but lay it down on the table nearest to him or her.

These rules were applied with the utmost strictness well into the modern era, as one former maid at Kensington Palace explained:

> I worked for Princess Margaret in the 1950s and it was made very clear to me that I was not to look at Margaret or to speak unless I was spoken to. If I met her in a corridor, I was to move aside and look down. I was supposed to put things down on a table near Margaret and then discreetly withdraw.
>
> She would tear you off a strip if you did anything she didn't like, but she could also be very kind. She bit my head off once – I can't remember why, but I had muddled something. Anyway, I was very young at the time and felt instantly tearful. She must

have noticed because she said, 'Take no notice of me. I'm just a bad-tempered old devil who can't help it.' I've never forgotten that because it was the only time I saw her more vulnerable side.

The fixed belief in the royal family and among the aristocracy was that the lower orders were inherently inferior; there was a feeling too that the great unwashed were always on the verge of insurrection, that if they were given an inch, they would take a mile or maybe even take over the whole country.

The nobility had seen what had happened during the French Revolution and they did not like it. Even a tough old bird such as the Duke of Wellington had a profound mistrust of his own army, or at least that part of it drawn from the lower classes. On being asked if he thought the French were afraid of his soldiers, the Duke famously replied, 'I don't know what effect these men will have upon the enemy, but, by God, they frighten me.'

The view of ordinary people as inherently dangerous if they were not kept under tight control created a division in the royal staff between those who accepted their place and those who did not.

In a conversation with the present author, the late Julia Power, whose grandmother worked at Windsor Castle and then at Buckingham Palace at the end of the nineteenth century, explained how the below-stairs world was split between the subservient and what she called the 'toughs'; the subservient accepted fully the idea that their employers were inherently superior; the toughs did not.

Grandma used to say that the younger staff at Buckingham

Palace tended to be less subservient – they didn't like the constant pressure to behave well and to work longer hours than we were paid for. The older staff, and especially those who were senior, were usually on the side of the royals – they gained some status by being higher than the new staff and they didn't want to lose it. The girls in the kitchens, the maids and cleaning staff, they wanted a bit of fun. My grandmother's great friend Elsie was told that while she worked in the palace, she was never to visit the music hall or a pub or a dance hall. Elsie was furious, so she went even more often to the music hall after that. But others devoted their lives to the royals, working longer than they needed to and, in some cases, not taking any time off at all. They were completely brainwashed!

Of course, it was more complicated for senior staff, for whom royal service had become a career that might give them security for life, a title and the chance to rise to a position that commanded respect both within the palace walls and outside.

The staff also knew that as you rose through the ranks, you were given jobs that offered more money for less work. And even if this was not the case, you might easily delegate most of your work to those below you. This was especially true of jobs held by the more aristocratic servants – the comptroller of the household, for example. The more staff he had at his command, the better he liked it, but there were limits and those limits were reached around halfway through Queen Victoria's long reign.

Prince Albert's favourite courtier, Baron Stockmar, shocked at the huge numbers of staff who had little to do but be at the command of the comptroller and other senior staff, determined (against staunch opposition) to do something about it.

On looking into the way Victoria's palaces were run, Stockmar grew increasingly angry. The methodical, logical German raged after being told that whenever a fire had to be lit in the palace dining room, the Lord Steward was responsible for laying the fire while the Lord Chamberlain's men had the task of actually lighting it.

Equally byzantine arrangements existed for the doors and windows – the servants who oiled the door hinges could not be asked, for example, to repair a pane of glass; those who repaired a pane of glass were not responsible for sweeping up the broken pieces of the glass that needed to be replaced.

The further Stockmar looked, the more extraordinary the staffing situation and management of the household seemed to be. He discovered, for instance, that the Lord Chamberlain was in charge of the pages, the housekeepers and maids, but the footmen reported to the Master of the Horse and the kitchen maids reported to the Lord Steward. Stockmar managed to rationalise some of these bizarre arrangements, but with Victoria resistant at every stage, it proved impossible to effect wholesale reform.

* * *

By the end of Victoria's reign, the main means by which servants were controlled was the threat of dismissal without what was called 'a character' – in modern parlance, without a reference. Given that the only opportunity for work for girls and young women in most areas of the country was domestic service, losing your 'character' was a disaster; the threat of losing it was a powerful incentive not to kick over the traces. And this was particularly true if you worked for the royal family.

It's easy to imagine that in earlier centuries punishments beyond a bad reference were far harsher, but in fact that is not the case.

In *Masters and Servants in Tudor England*, Alison Sim explains that in the late sixteenth century, below-stairs servants who misbehaved were first given a warning; for a second offence, food and wages might be withheld and only as a last resort would a servant lose their job. Corporal punishment seems to have been resorted to less often than we might imagine, though no doubt an exasperated cook might occasionally clout a kitchen boy or maid. Curiously, before the Reformation one of the more serious offences for kitchen and other domestic staff was swearing – but specifically swearing by the Mass.

But whatever the restrictions and difficulties of being a servant in the royal family, things were often far worse elsewhere, even if one happened to be working for an aristocrat.

One former royal servant interviewed by the present author recalled moving from London in the 1930s where he had worked at Buckingham Palace back to Shropshire after his father became ill. He began work in a large house owned by the local lord of the manor.

I was amazed when [his butler] showed me where I was to sleep – it was in the cellar and so damp that you could see trickles of moisture running down the walls. I told the butler I wasn't prepared to take the job as I'd had my own room in Buckingham Palace. He wasn't moved in the slightest and we parted on bad terms and I found a job somewhere else.

Even men of the church who might have recalled Jesus's instruction 'give all thou hast to the poor' tended to treat their servants as if they were pack animals. The writer and artist Denys Watkins Pitchford, interviewed by the present author, explained how his father, the Vicar of Lamport in Northamptonshire, would sit close to the fire and the log basket on a cold winter's night: 'When the fire needed to be stirred up or another log added, he would ring for the fourteen-year-old maid to come up two flights of stairs just to throw another log on the fire.'

It was all a matter of status, and the obsession with status among the servants themselves often meant they made life unnecessarily difficult for each other. Retired maid Rose Plummer recalled how 'the third housemaid had to always open the door for the second housemaid, who in turn opened the door for the first housemaid. If you went into a room at the palace to clean in the wrong order, there was hell to pay.'

* * *

By the early twentieth century, religion played a lesser part in servant life, but in most big houses and certainly in the royal palaces attendance at church had always been obligatory, along with prayers once a week, or even every morning in the houses of the devout. In the early modern period in royal palaces – Whitehall, Eltham and St James – Mass would have been celebrated every day in many different rooms. There were portable altars and large numbers of permanently employed religious staff.

Over the centuries, and especially after the Reformation, the numbers of religious staff declined, and obligatory attendance at daily or even weekly prayers had largely vanished by the mid-twentieth century. This decline was matched, at least in the twentieth century, by a steep decline in the appeal of jobs in domestic service even if those jobs meant working for the royal family.

After the Great War, during which women proved they were just as good at jobs traditionally reserved for men, girls abandoned domestic service in their droves and although the royal family was still able to recruit sufficient numbers to work in the kitchens (and young men to work as pages and footmen), the great servant shift did not go unnoticed.

The *Daily Mail* complained that the housewives of England had been cruelly abandoned and that no social security should be paid to girls who had been made redundant from factory work but did not wish to return to domestic service.

It never seems to have occurred to the *Daily Mail* and many others that housewives were not automatically entitled to be idle and to employ people to do work they could quite easily do themselves. But what began to be called the 'shame of cap and apron' among domestic staff extended from the highest to the lowest. In 1844, Mary Ann Ashford published *Life of a Licensed*

Victualler's Daughter, which describes her life as a servant. She recalls how she was pushed into the kitchen one day while at home so as not to embarrass her relatives, who considered she had let the family down by becoming a servant.

That the tide had turned can also be judged by the fact that throughout the nineteenth century *Punch* magazine had regularly mocked servants who tried to be more genteel; who aped, as *Punch* put it, the manners and accents of their employers, especially the royal family. But then towards the end of the nineteenth century and on into the early years of the twentieth century, something extraordinary happened. For the first time in history, the aristocracy and members of the royal family found themselves mocked and for the very thing on which they had always prided themselves: their idleness.

Britain's landowning class feared revolution was on the way when Chancellor of the Exchequer David Lloyd George stood up in Parliament in 1909 and railed against the aristocracy, describing them as 'the permanently unemployed' and as 'parasites'.

By the 1920s, so much had changed that novelist and poet Thomas Hardy was able to write his poem 'The Ruined Maid'. 'Ruined' was a dreaded word to a Victorian audience – it meant that a woman had lost her 'good name', meaning she had become pregnant while unmarried or had become a kept mistress. Hardy makes the point clearly enough that being kept in fine clothes and fine foods by becoming a rich man's mistress (and thereby escaping the shame of cap and apron) was well worth the loss of reputation.

'O 'Melia, my dear, this does everything crown!
Who could have supposed I should meet you in Town?
And whence such fair garments, such prosperity?' —
'O didn't you know I'd been ruined?' said she.

— 'You left us in tatters, without shoes or socks,
Tired of digging potatoes, and spudding up docks;
And now you've gay bracelets and bright feathers three!' —
'Yes: that's how we dress when we're ruined,' said she.

Few would have described a royal mistress as 'ruined', which speaks volumes about the hypocrisy and moral confusion of the Victorians and Edwardians. Edward VII's mistress Alice Keppel was feted in high society and almost never criticised, whereas a middle-class or working-class girl living as a mistress would have been shunned and ostracised. We know that despite herself being someone's mistress, Alice Keppel even sacked one of her servants when she discovered the girl had what was then called a 'follower', in other words a boyfriend. The idea that this might be seen as extraordinarily hypocritical would never have occurred to Alice Keppel; there was one rule for the rich and another for the poor. It was as if a servant girl and her mistress were two different species.

As we move into the modern era, the idea of losing one's good name became less important as young women were able to choose different kinds of work. The 'shame of cap and apron' shifted; increasingly, the upper classes were shocked to find that their mode of life, their proud idleness, was less something to be

admired and more something perhaps to be ashamed of. Henrietta Litchfield, the daughter of Charles Darwin, confessed at the
age of ninety that she had never made a pot of tea (or anything
ese) in her life. Her Victorian upbringing made her feel this was
perfectly natural for a woman of her class, but she had lived into
an age in which such idleness was no longer admired. And there
was another problem with relying on servants to do everything.
By the 1920s, women such as Henrietta, and indeed members of
the royal family, suddenly found their domestics had abandoned
them for work in factories. Power had shifted and women who
could not look after themselves had to offer all sorts of induce-
ments to employ and retain domestics, as Julia Power recalled
her grandmother saying:

After the Great War, the royal family was still able to keep just as
many servants as they had ever had because there was still a lot
of status involved with working for the royals in any capacity. But
aristocratic families and even minor royals struggled to engage
and keep servants, especially female servants. They much preferred working in factories – the pay was better, they could gossip
with their friends and no one tried to control whether or not
they had boyfriends or what they did in their free time. Best of
all, rather than one afternoon a week off from work they had half
a day on Saturday and the whole of Sunday; they were suddenly
free. I stayed working as a domestic for my minor royal – she was
the last granddaughter of Queen Victoria – because I felt sorry
for her, but also because she increased my pay, reduced my hours
and began now and then even to speak to me! I couldn't believe

it. At one time she would never have spoken to me or acknowledged my existence – messages would have reached the kitchen at Kensington Palace via a footman, the butler or the housekeeper or chef, but never directly to me.

Then one day I happened to be somewhere I really shouldn't have been – one of the sitting rooms – when she was there. She asked me my name and was clearly making an effort to remember it because when I gave notice six months later, she asked to see me and tried very gently to persuade me to stay. When I said I couldn't stay, she almost seemed to have tears in her eyes. The ogres had turned into the gentle and considerate. It was a real revolution.

Chapter Eight

Intimate arrangements: the royal bowels and the Groom of the Stool

———————

'Do you still throw spears at each other?'
– PRINCE PHILIP, DUKE OF EDINBURGH, ON MEETING
A GROUP OF INDIGENOUS AUSTRALIANS

*'Philip used regularly to leave small presents on Elizabeth's bed,
little jokey presents, like a pair of rubber gloves
before they went to Balmoral.'*
– RETIRED BUCKINGHAM PALACE MAID

Such was the almost holy aura that surrounded the monarch in the late medieval and early modern periods that kings and queens were seen quite literally as God's anointed. Before the Reformation, only the Pope could face down a king; after Henry VIII's break with Rome, kings and queens in England became the ultimate source of both religious and secular power.

This created a curious situation where even the royal bowels were hallowed. If the king was God's chosen one then even his excrement had to be treated with dignity and respect – and thus came into being the servant role known as the Groom of the Stool, perhaps the most bizarre servant role in the history of the monarchy.

It was the Groom of the Stool's job to oversee the monarch's lavatorial exploits and although we are still not certain that the Groom of the Stool (or, officially, Groom of the King's Close Stool) had actually to clean the monarch after his ablutions, it is very possible that this was indeed part of his work.

Certainly, at the very least he would have been on hand to pass towels and sponges to the king and to remove the close stool (a sort of portable commode) after the king had finished. William III's late-seventeenth-century velvet-covered close stool still exists and is held in the Royal Collection.

According to *The Book of Nurture*, published in 1452, the Groom of the Stool had to 'look there be blanket, cotton, or linen to wipe the nether end, and ever he calls, wait ready and prompt'.

This does rather suggest that the Groom of the Stool's role really was extraordinarily intimate.

We should remember too that in an era when testing urine and faeces for signs of illness was central to medicine, the groom had a vitally important role. He, it might be assumed, would be the first to notice if anything was amiss and indeed, we know that the last of Henry VIII's Grooms of the Stool, Sir Anthony Denny, was the man who told Henry in 1547 that he was dying. The groom was so important that he was also known as First

Gentleman of the Chamber. Under Henry VII, he had begun to be given dual responsibilities: Groom of the Stool was combined with the role of Keeper of the Privy Purse. Presumably the argument went something along the lines: if you could be trusted with the monarch's bowel movements, you could be trusted with his money.

But the Groom of the Stool was just one among a number of servants who dealt with the most intimate and secret aspects of a monarch's life and it is certainly true that, over time, the role became less intimate, as did so many royal servant roles. In fact, almost all intimate royal servant roles became less intimate over the centuries, not just because it began to be clear that the monarch could do things without assistance – that may have been a major leap of faith – but also because monarchs grew increasingly fed up with having no privacy. The extent to which they were public property until relatively recently can be judged by the wedding night of George II and Princess Caroline of Brandenburg-Ansbach in 1705. As they went to bed, dressed only in their nightshirts, the couple found themselves surrounded by courtiers, lords, ladies, servants and even strangers who watched them climb nervously into bed and then made extremely bawdy remarks until ushered out of the room.

* * *

So far, we have only really looked at male monarchs. Queens did not employ a Groom of the Stool, but their intimate needs were met by a female equivalent. Elizabeth I had her Lady of the Bedchamber, and all female monarchs have always employed teams of ladies in waiting, drawn from the aristocratic pool. Ladies in waiting were always just companion ornaments; being aristocrats, they had no practical duties. The tasks of supplying towels, making beds, emptying close stools and cleaning and tidying was left to female servants of a lower order.

The Lady of the Bedchamber role was always filled by the wife of a lord and although she might on occasion actually help the monarch wash and dress, she usually directed the other, less socially elevated women of the bedchamber to carry out the menial tasks.

The obsession with hierarchy and what was seen as the natural order meant that the queen could not be expected to direct servants who were not in the social stratum immediately below her own. She needed an aristocratic woman to pass the message down to a woman from the gentry, who would in turn pass it down to the maids and other lower-class staff.

The employment of women as ladies of the bed chamber and ladies in waiting, often a dozen or more at a time, continued until the modern era – in fact, right up until Charles III's wife Queen Camilla abolished the role of lady in waiting in 2023.

Under Elizabeth II, the traditions associated with the role of ladies in waiting were almost unchanged from centuries earlier: all Elizabeth's and her sister Margaret's ladies in waiting, including perhaps most famously the author Anne Glenconner, were aristocrats who, like the Queen herself, grew up in an era during which the old natural order was simply taken for granted, as it had been for at least 600 years.

Working from the Eltham Ordinances, a rulebook put together in the fifteenth century to reduce the chaos at the English court by laying down basic rules for servants, the historian Alison Sim, in *Masters and Servants in Tudor England*, gives us a neat summary of what would have happened each day in the royal bedroom in the mid-sixteenth century:

> The two gentlemen of the privy chamber who were on duty had to be up by 7am at the latest or sooner if the king had told them he wanted to be up earlier. Only the gentlemen were allowed to lay hands on his royal person so obviously they had to be up and ready dressed by the time the king wished to rise. The yeomen of the wardrobe would bring the king's clothes as far as the privy chamber door, but they were not allowed to enter. Instead, they passed the royal clothes to the gentlemen of the bedchamber. In the same way, if the king wanted a snack between meals, food and drink were brought to the privy chamber and then handed to the gentlemen to give to the king.

The ordinances also explain that aside from the Esquires of the Bedchamber, 'no man else [is] to sett hand on the king'.

The king's private apartments must have been very crowded at times, because in addition to the servants of the body there were the yeoman ushers to guard the doors, pages to light fires, and teams of grooms to tidy and to put up beds each night for all the intimate servants to sleep on. These beds all had to be taken down and moved out of the way each morning.

Echoes of this world continued well into the twentieth

century. When William Tallon, Page of the Backstairs, arrived at the late Queen Mother's bedroom at Clarence House each morning – and he hardly missed a day from the 1960s to the mid-1990s – he carried a tray with tea and the Queen Mother's favourite biscuits but he was not allowed to enter the bedroom itself. He would knock and then hand the tray through the door to one of Elizabeth's female staff.

Like her daughter Elizabeth II, the Queen Mother was always woken by female staff and neither she nor her daughter would have dreamt of getting fed, washed and dressed on their own. Having been helped every day of their lives, they simply took it for granted that dressing was a tricky matter not to be attempted unaided. Of course, neither of the two Elizabeths would have been taken to the lavatory by their intimate servants, but the servant's role of dresser had come to mean something only slightly different more than 500 years after the death of Henry VIII. Henry would have been lifted, squeezed and folded into his clothes by the gentlemen of the bedchamber. For Elizabeth, her clothes were designed by Angela Kelly and laid out each morning by Bobo MacDonald, who then helped the Queen get into them.

Angela Kelly was Elizabeth II's official dresser for more than twenty years – she worked for the Queen from 1994 until the latter's final illness – and we know from her autobiography, *The Other Side of the Coin*, that her work involved designing outfits for the Queen but not actually slotting her into those outfits on a daily basis. Kelly was typical of modern servants or staff who work close to the modern royals. Even in the Queen's private apartments, her role was to advise and discuss, to prepare dresses and suits and then make sure they looked as the Queen wished them to look. Intimacy had vanished, from this as from all the other senior bedroom roles.

The only intimate servant Elizabeth II fully trusted was the woman who had looked after her every need when she was a child; Margaret 'Bobo' MacDonald helped the Queen into her clothes each day until she was too old and frail to continue. Bobo also sat with Elizabeth at teatime, eating jam rounds as they had eaten them together for more than half a century.

A retired Buckingham Palace maid recalled something of their relationship.

The Queen was never completely relaxed with anyone – except Margaret MacDonald. She had never known a time when they had not been together and though she, Margaret, came from a very humble background, I think the Queen would have parted with all her aristocratic advisers and friends and all her ladies in waiting rather than part with Margaret. We used to say they were joined at the hip!

Bedroom staff during the latter part of Elizabeth II's reign did not have to manage the monarch's thunder box in and out of her bedroom, but, as one former Buckingham Palace staffer explained:

The Queen still had to go to the lavatory, although I've met many people who find that almost impossible to believe! One thing I can tell you for sure – she always has her own lavatory that no one else ever uses. In fact, in all her palaces she has a loo that no one else ever uses, which has to be cleaned and kept in good order by the domestics. I remember when I started work thinking, 'I'm actually in the room where the Queen goes to the loo!' I almost shocked myself! The only other thing I can tell you is that the Queen liked wooden seats (she hated plastic) as well as old-fashioned scents and soaps in her bathroom and she adored baths and hated showers. She always used to wince when someone referred to perfume – she thought it an affectation. She always referred to perfumes as scent.

Bobo MacDonald told me that Elizabeth was almost always calm and usually quite formal, but she would very occasionally do something surprising. Bobo said Elizabeth liked throwing blocks of bath salt into her bath from the other side of the door into the bathroom – she was a very good shot apparently and never missed. And she liked to have one of her dogs, one of the corgis, in the bathroom with her and you could hear her talking to the dog all the while and throwing dog biscuits out of the bath while she was having a good soak. Bobo never said what the Queen said to the dog, but she insisted the Queen could occasionally be heard chuckling to herself.

In the secret world of the modern royal bedroom, there are still oddities to be taken into account – we know, for example that wherever Queen Elizabeth went during her long reign she was always accompanied by her own lavatory seat, carefully and discreetly stowed in her luggage. Occasionally, and especially on foreign tours, courtiers had to speak to civil servants, who had to speak to their opposite numbers abroad, and a whole new lavatory would be installed ready for the Queen's arrival.

Even royals slightly further down the scale from the monarch herself have their lavatorial peccadilloes. At a central London conference centre in 2004, news that the guest of honour was to be the Princess Royal, Princess Anne, was greeted with consternation because the lavatories in the conference centre were looking rather jaded. The solution was to completely replace one lavatory, including the plumbing, and forbid anyone else to use the new lavatory until after Princess Anne had attended the conference and left.

Other members of the royal family have their bathroom quirks too – in the case of King Charles, a member of his personal staff has the solemn duty each day of putting toothpaste on the royal toothbrush, and woe betide him if there is too little or too much toothpaste!

According to a former member of Charles's staff, the prince (as he then was) had always put his own toothpaste on his own brush until a polo injury meant someone else had to do it for him, but Charles enjoyed having it done so much that when he recovered the use of his arm, he kept quiet and the valet continued to dole out the toothpaste.

Being very particular about this sort of detail in a way that ordinary people find incomprehensible is central to the private lives of the senior royals, perhaps because it is all they have. Like royalty and the aristocracy in earlier times, modern princes are programmed from their earliest years to see their work (and perhaps also themselves!) as too important to allow them time to do the sort of dull domestic things most of us do for ourselves.

Suits must be pressed and laid out after a period of consultation the night before; shoes must be polished, ties chosen. Baths must be run at precisely the same time each day and both King Charles and the Prince of Wales, Prince William, are prone to tantrums if things are not done to their liking. 'They both get irritated very quickly,' said one former member of staff,

because throughout their lives they have had these things done for them, so they are very picky. It comes naturally to them. And people who have everything done for them from childhood tend to be rather spoiled and prone to bouts of irritation because they have no idea how much work is involved in washing and ironing, polishing and sewing when they have never done any of it themselves. I don't know where William would be without Kate – she hasn't had everything done for her throughout her life, so she calms him down when he gets a bit fractious. She says he sometimes has to be treated as her fourth child!

Bedroom and bathroom staff in the modern royal world are simply carefully vetted members of the public – ordinary people – who have applied for a job at the palace. Centuries ago, these more intimate jobs, as we have seen, were never given to ordinary people because that did not accord with the medieval and early modern notion of the natural order of things: if the king was second only to God, then it would be going against the natural order for his personal attendants to be drawn from anything other than the next closest level in the social hierarchy, the nobility.

In the twenty-first century, members of the nobility are still employed by the royals, but only as advisers. If they are already friends of the monarch, the job will come with royal perks – a grace and favour apartment, perhaps, or an honorary title that allows the monarch to pay a salary.

When the role of Groom of the Stool morphed into an advisory role, the name changed. The word 'stool' became an embarrassing reminder that this socially elevated job had rather lowly origins, so that had to change, and under Queen Victoria it did change: the Groom of the Stool found himself known as the Groom of the Stole, which suggested a more refined responsibility for clothing rather than handing over sponges and towels for the royal nether regions.

Intimate contact with the monarch, now and in the past, led often to friendship, however guarded that friendship might sometimes be. Having an aristocratic background gave the Groom of the Stole and all other aristocratic servants the chance to give advice, to sympathise and to make suggestions – clearly this happened often and the rewards for getting it right were considerable. Sir William Compton, for example, was Henry VIII's Groom of the Stool from 1509 to 1526. He had been page to the young Henry and following his appointment as Henry VIII's first Groom of the Stool he obtained favours for his friends and became one of the king's closest, most trusted advisers. His reward was a string of preferments that made him a rich man – he became Chancellor of Ireland and Ranger of Windsor

Great Park among a string of other titles. None of these titles involved any work; they were simply a means for Henry to make his favoured servant rich, and the Compton family today is still hugely wealthy and living in their vast ancestral home, Compton Wynyates in Warwickshire.

The key to Compton's success was that he did as he was told, despite any moral qualms he may have had. So, in addition to attending to the monarch's lavatorial needs, he spent much of his career procuring women for the king – a role that many royal servants have performed down to the modern era. Page of the Bedchamber Thomas Chaffinch's main role was to procure women for Charles II, for example, and in the ultimate act of bedroom service for one's king, George Keppel, from whom Queen Camilla is descended, procured his own wife, Alice Keppel, for Edward VII.

* * *

The earliest record we have for a Groom of the Stool comes from the 1400s, during the reign of Henry VI, and in an example of longevity that typifies royal servant roles, it wasn't formally abolished until 1901, when Edward VII acceded to the throne.

Grooms of the Stool have included Charles Spencer, an ancestor of Diana, Princess of Wales – he was Groom of the Stool to George I from 1719 to 1722 – and Willem van Keppel (from whom Camilla is also descended), who was Groom of the Stool to George II from 1751 to 1755.

Money and status were, as we have seen, the great attractions of royal service in any role, but for all servants in the early modern period there was an attraction in addition to financial reward: noble servants attached to the monarch's private rooms were often rewarded with the monarch's old clothes.

This may not sound much in the twenty-first century, but in an age when all clothing had to be made by hand, fine clothes were extremely expensive. The finest, most expensive clothing of all was worn by the monarch and inheriting a monarch's cast-offs was the equivalent of a modern banker's Christmas bonus. Royal clothes were made with silver and gold thread and the finest silks and satins; in terms of value, the best dresses and coats would have been equivalent to several years' salary for a page, and fine clothes given to you by the monarch were a way of signalling to everyone at court that you were someone of consequence.

In addition to dressing the king, the servants with the most intimate jobs – the esquires of the body – helped the king bathe. There is a myth that people in the early modern period never bathed. It is certainly true that ordinary people did not bathe in the modern sense of immersing themselves in a bath or standing under a shower. The practicalities for the poor were insuperable, but there is a good deal of evidence that monarchs did indeed bathe.

In his book *The Royal Palaces of Tudor England*, Simon Thurley quotes from F. J. Furnivall's *Manners and Meals in Olden Time*, published in 1868. The book is a collection of early accounts of Tudor life and includes the following account of preparing the king's bath: 'Hang sheet round about ye roof, do thus as ye mean every sheet full of flowers and herbes soote [sweet] and green and look you have sponges five or six thereon your sovereign to sit … and so he may bathe him there.'

One of the most difficult things to appreciate as we look back from the twenty-first century is how grubby people were in earlier centuries. Deodorants were not widely available until the 1950s and most of the population owned only the clothes they stood up in, with perhaps a small amount of spare linen and a winter coat. The very wealthy owned more clothing, far more in the case of royalty, but washing using hot water and soap did not happen.

Stone baths existed at Hampton Court and although there is no direct evidence that Wolsey (for whom the palace was first built) or Henry VIII actually used them, it seems improbable that they remained entirely unused, especially as cleanliness was a religious imperative ('cleanliness is next to godliness'). Remains of a sunken bath have also been discovered at Whitehall in the buried ruins of the old palace that burned down in 1698. Certainly, Charles II's favourite courtier, John Wilmot, Earl of Rochester, exhorted his wives and mistresses to 'use sponges for before and papers for behind'.

No doubt the very wealthy also bathed occasionally, but as Ian Mortimer explains in *The Time Traveller's Guide to the Middle Ages*, many if not most of those who bathed made sure they kept their underwear on while they did it – so even the esquires of the body may not have been permitted to see their sovereign entirely naked.

For the royal servants, close stools and baths were available only for the most aristocratic – senior servants who themselves employed their own servants to empty and clean for them. Lower down the social scale, lavatories were provided, although in most cases only at the great palaces. We know there was a fourteen-seat lavatory at Hampton Court, for example, but no monarch would have used this.

Urinating was a different matter and for monarchs and others it was not something to be embarrassed about or even in many cases something to do in private. At Hampton Court Palace, in the various courtyards we see today, red crosses were once painted up to and above waist height to stop men urinating against the walls: the idea was that no one would dare urinate on the sign of the cross. But royal servants often urinated in the corner of rooms or inside their enormous chimneys. Andrew Boord, whose book *The Brevyary of Healthe* was published in 1547, warns, 'beware of pissing in chymnes', but the practice continued because 'making water' seemed harmless and few wanted to venture too far from the fire on a cold winter evening.

But change did come and by the time we reach the Georgian era, buckets and chamber pots were provided for all lavatorial needs, hidden, for example at Kensington Palace, in tiny rooms like broom cupboards concealed behind fireplaces in the thickness of the walls. Bodily functions, even royal bodily functions, were gradually becoming subject to an increasing obsession with gentility, privacy and decorum – a process that led eventually to the prudery of the Victorian era, during which the well-born almost convinced themselves that bodily functions didn't exist.

The influence of twentieth-century ideas about egalitarianism and elitism took their toll and when Queen Victoria's granddaughter Princess Marie Louise published her book, *Memories of Six Reigns*, in 1960, she was at pains to explain that although she and each of her sisters had had their own lady's maid from when they were small children, they had also been taught 'how to dress ourselves, to fold our clothes and to tidy our beds and bathrooms'.

It was her nod to the changed world.

None of her ancestors would have admitted to knowing how to carry out such menial tasks. And even Princess Marie Louise would not have been so eager to boast a knowledge of cleaning and cooking – that would have been a step too far even for the twentieth century.

Chapter Nine

Food, glorious food: eating, drinking and making merry

Daily life for servants in the royal palaces ran – and still runs – like clockwork, but there were always two worlds running in parallel. Nurses and nannies would look after the royal children in the nursery; the other servants would run everything else. Kitchen maids and other maids only rarely moved into the nursery; likewise, footmen. A nursery footman was a very different creature from an ordinary footman, as a former Buckingham Palace maid recalled:

Nursery footmen were always seen as a cut above the rest – they had to be just that bit more genteel as they worked closely with the royal children. Nursery maids were the same. I have no idea what little clues the senior staff were looking for when they made their choice – sometimes I think it was just good looks. A nice-looking young man was always more likely to be offered a nursery footman's role and it was the same with the nursery maids. The pretty ones got the job. We used to joke that the rest of us were so ugly we might give the princesses nightmares!

The royal nurseries were always beautifully decorated and the royal children lived in luxury, but some nursery practices came to seem barbaric. It was standard practice in the nursery until the 1950s, for example, for the nursery nannies to administer patent medicines containing small quantities of laudanum; Elizabeth II's father George VI was dosed with it as a baby, as was his brother Edward VIII. Another favoured nursery medicine was known as Daffy's Elixir and it was popular because it contained significant quantities of alcohol.

For the young princes and princesses, every meal was had in the nursery, with the nursery maids, the nursery footmen and the nannies all in attendance, right up until they were considered old enough to eat properly at their parents' table.

Eating has always been of enormous importance to the royals. Every day of their lives, members of the royal family – and indeed of the aristocracy – would wear one set of clothes during the day and then dress specially for dinner in the evening. Royal dinners were and are central to the role of monarchy. Important visitors and especially heads of state are always invited to dine at the various royal palaces.

It is difficult to conceive of the scale of the kitchen operation at the royal palaces and this is especially true when we consider earlier centuries when eating and drinking were even more important to daily life at court than they have been in modern times.

Banquets and feasts were designed to impress, but even when a monarch dined with his or her family or dined alone, food had to be expensive, elaborate and painstakingly prepared. As with clothes, palaces and furniture, food had to be the best money could buy – and there had to be lots of it. What was expensive and elaborate in the normal course of events became extraordinarily so when ambassadors or other visitors arrived at court. The point was that the ambassadors should report back to their own monarchs on the magnificence of the English court.

But that magnificence did not include regular meals for the staff, or at least not the kitchen staff. In the early modern period, for example, the kitchen staff who slept in the royal palaces did not eat breakfast at all. Edward IV's mother, Cecily, Duchess of York, was the first member of the royal family to try to create a code of conduct for the court. Probably compiled in the 1470s by Cecily's secretary Robert Incent, her code insists that 'breakfasts be there none, saving onely the head officers when they be present; to the ladyes and gentlewomen, to the deane and to the chappell, to the almoner, to the cofferer, to the clerk of the kitchen, to the gentlemen ushers and to the marshall'.

Because the staff began work so early, dinner – what would

now be called lunch – was served remarkably early, probably mid-morning or even earlier, although the monarch of course ate whenever he chose.

And as with all aspects of a monarch's daily life, eating was surrounded by ceremony. According to the Earl of Huntingdon's ordinances, first published in 1790, an usher was to 'cause all men in the hall to come to the side of the hall and be bare-headed while their honour's meat passeth through'.

Food, like clothing, was also linked to status, as the following from the same ordinances reveals:

The excess of diet and provisions had become so great, and the consequences were likely to prove so detrimental to the nation, that King Edward II in the 8th year of his Reign, found it necessary to issue a proclamation to restrain it. This Ordinance stated that, by the outrageous and excessive multitude of meats and dishes, which the great men of the kingdom used in their castles, and by persons of inferior rank imitating their example, beyond what their stations required and their circumstances could afford, many great evils had come upon the kingdom; the health of the King's subjects had been injured, their property consumed, and they had been reduced to poverty; but the King being desirous to put a stop to such excesses, with the advice and consent of his Great Council, had ordained: that the great men of the kingdom should have only two courses of flesh meats served up to their tables; each course consisting only of two kinds of flesh meat: except Prelates, Earls, Barons, and the great men of the land, who might have an inter-meat … of one kind of meat if they pleased.

It's difficult to imagine King Charles III imposing restrictions on who eats what in his kingdom in this way, but magnificent royal banquets in the twenty-first century are not in essentials unlike royal banquets four centuries earlier.

It is often argued that in the early modern period, hygiene and cleanliness were almost unheard of; in fact, great efforts were made in the royal palaces to ensure food was not contaminated. Royal ordinances forbade, for example, defecating and urinating in or near the kitchens – even in the medieval period, people were aware that this was decidedly unhealthy. In his 1542 treatise *A Compendyous Regyment, or a Dyetary of Healthe*, Andrew Boorde insists that 'houses of easement' (i.e. lavatories) must be kept well away from places where people eat and sleep.

Royal kitchens have always been crowded places. But centuries ago, the royal court was far bigger than in modern times and preparing food was far more elaborate and time-consuming. In a royal kitchen, work virtually never stopped. The scullery maids and kitchen boys hardly ever left the kitchen. Indeed, work started so early in the morning that it was often scarcely worth going to bed. According to the Eltham Ordinances, the lower kitchen staff began to light the kitchen fires in summer at four or five o'clock; other staff began work soon after this and even the well-born pages had to be up by 7 a.m.

The lowest kitchen servants – maids and kitchen boys – slept on the kitchen floor until well into the eighteenth century, and given the size of extant royal kitchens – at Hampton Court, for example – this would not have been difficult. They would use a palliasse (a kind of cheap straw mattress) which could easily be put away in the morning. (Incidentally, the phrase 'hit the sack' comes from the fact that a palliasse had to be beaten with a stick each night to even out the straw and make it comfortable enough to sleep on.)

Even those slightly more senior servants who might have access to a bed were expected to share that bed. Sleeping in the kitchen was not the hardship it might seem today – the kitchen was, after all, usually the warmest room in the palace. Although staff dormitories and then individual rooms were eventually provided in Buckingham Palace by the mid-twentieth century, they were almost always very cold.

Grace Williams, who worked for the royal family as a maid, recalled her room at Buckingham Palace just after the First World War:

Oh, heavens, it was cold and the palace was so huge that it took me weeks helped by another girl even to work out how to get back to my room each evening. I was always getting lost! My room, which I shared, seemed miles away from the kitchen – such a long walk, and Buckingham Palace is designed so that servants were to use passages and staircases never used by the royal family. They were cold and drab and unheated, unlike the main staircases and corridors, which were carpeted and magnificent.

But as Grace also pointed out, conditions were far worse for maids of all work in small middle-class houses.

> No one wanted to work for middle-class people because they treated you so badly – in the palace, you were more or less anonymous, you see, and you might be shouted at by the chef but there was nothing personal about it. She or he – the palace liked to have male chefs – was also an employee, but in a semi-detached out in Pinner or wherever, the mistress was often nasty because she owned the house and paid your wages and she resented every penny because she was bored and had nothing to do except find fault.

* * *

By the time Queen Victoria ascended the throne, the monarch had lost the power to wage war or to have much say at all in the running of the country, although Victoria often behaved as if no one had yet dared tell her this was the case. The result was that ritual, including the ritual of dining, became ever more important and not just because banquets were a way of welcoming visiting dignitaries. Food for both Queen Victoria and her son Edward VII was central to their lives, as Annie Gray explains in her 2017 book *The Greedy Queen*.

Gray agrees with all Victoria's modern biographers that Victoria gorged herself and became 'plump as a partridge', but her son was if anything worse: there is a wonderful if perhaps apocryphal story of Edward's wife Alexandra laughing as she watched Bertie climb into his carriage with his mistress Mrs Keppel. They were both so fat that the coachman had to lean on the outside of the door with all his weight in order to close it before they could set off.

The temptations of eating were always greater for royalty, who, at any time of the day or night, might contact the kitchen staff and demand to be fed. And as Annie Gray points out, the kitchen was always ready to prepare anything from a 400lb side of beef to the milk puddings Victoria so loved. It is perhaps no wonder then that Henry VIII was grossly obese towards the end of his life, Queen Mary gorged on chocolate, Queen Anne was nicknamed 'brandy nan' and Elizabeth I consumed so much sugar, her teeth rotted.

*   *   *

Some kitchen and other domestic jobs have changed or vanished – the palace chandler, for example, was responsible for candles, tapers, rushlights and other forms of lighting. Candles, like food, were socially stratified: the best beeswax candles were supplied to the noble servants and the royal family, while the lower servants had to make do with tallow – animal fat candles that worked well enough but smoked horribly and smelled badly.

Clothing was similarly socially stratified: lace and silk were the preserve of the courtiers and members of the royal family, while coarse woollen clothing was given to the servants, though even the lowliest kitchen servants might expect a new set of clothes once or perhaps twice a year. But lower servants would have had only one set of clothes at any one time.

Cooks were given money to buy their own clothes and those of the lower servants. In 1541, according to the Eltham Ordinances, the head cook was given twenty marks to buy clothing for the scullions and 'galapines', as the kitchen boys were known.

Working long hours with little chance to wash and a change of clothes once or at most twice a year, the kitchen boys (and the cooks and other kitchen staff too) would have been very dirty – the ordinances specifically mention the need for new clothes so that the boys avoided 'such uncleanness as may be the annoyance of those by whom they shall passe', but it is difficult to believe a change of clothes once or even twice a year would make much difference.

Throughout servant history there has also been a gulf between what the royal family ate and what was eaten by their staff. The toughest parts of any meat were always given to the servants – cuts that needed to be boiled – while roasted joints were reserved for the courtiers and the king's family.

All meals were to some extent banquets, because for the royal family almost everything was steeped in ceremonial; because good food elaborately prepared was a sign of status, nothing could be rushed. Like clothes, food was expensive and good food was very expensive. A quick meal would have been unimaginable. And if ordinary meals were elaborate affairs, banquets were sometimes extraordinary.

During a visit to England by the French ambassador, Cardinal Wolsey organised a meal that included a model of St Paul's

Cathedral made entirely from sugar, together with a sugar chess board which had a specially built case so it could be taken safely back to France.

Even simple meals for the royals were not simple at all: they would include numerous meat courses, one of which would often be a large bird, perhaps a swan, and in order to create an impression, the swan might well have been cooked with a goose inside it, which in turn contained a duck and so on down to a partridge or some other small bird. Another favourite dish was a chicken containing eggs at various stages of development inside it.

According to the Eltham Ordinances, a meal for the noble members of the household would typically include chicken, rabbit, beef, mutton and veal followed by a second course of wildfowl – duck, goose and perhaps swan – as well as yet more chicken, and pigeon. After that, sugary puddings and tarts would be eaten together with butter – butter was eaten with a spoon, rather as we would eat yoghurt today.

Vegetables, especially root vegetables and beans, were considered largely the food of the poor, so very few were eaten by the nobility and only rarely in quantity, although salads were popular.

Elizabeth I was convinced that for her breath always to smell sweet she must eat sweet foods – which she did in large quantities. So much so that visitors to the court noted that as she aged, her teeth turned black, and we know she suffered regularly with toothache.

But the point of inviting guests to eat with the royal family, then as in the twenty-first century, was to delight and impress;

modern monarchs have been just as eager to impress as Tudor kings.

According to a retired footman interviewed by the present author,

Queen Elizabeth II always personally oversaw the laying of the fifty-metre banqueting table in St George's Hall, Windsor Castle. The table can seat 160 and banquets for visitors are so important that a footman is employed to measure the precise distance between every knife, plate and fork, place decoration, bouquet and vase. So big is the table at Windsor that the footman wears special felt-soled shoes so that he is able climb up on the table and walk up and down between the place settings rather than constantly have to walk all the way around to move things.

The footman used to slide about the table top between the complicated place settings, the flower vases and so on and he never upset a thing. He was brilliant at it. The Queen loved to be involved and I heard her once say to the footman on the table, 'It's rather like skating, isn't it, but not on thin ice?'

At Buckingham Palace, where state banquets are more often held, the banqueting room can seat 170 guests at a horseshoe-shaped table.

Hundreds of chefs, maids, footmen and other domestic staff are needed to make a royal banquet run like clockwork. In 1900, a kitchen maid might be paid £10 a year; a chef, by contrast, might have an annual salary of £200, such was the value placed on food. In the twenty-first century, wages for kitchen staff have not improved that much, with the maids being paid little above the legal minimum wage, which in 2024 was just under £11.50 per hour.

Always underpaid and overworked – a tradition in domestic service – the royal kitchen staff often supplemented their meagre wages by helping themselves to plates and cutlery if they could get away with it.

One former member of the kitchen staff interviewed by the present author recalled:

In the 1970s, students often worked in the palace kitchen in the summer when things were busy. We were never vetted because it was assumed we would never have access to anything important and there was a sort of weird idea that no one would dare do anything illegal or unlawful if it involved royalty. But we were so badly paid that many of us stole almost automatically and of course much of the cutlery was solid silver so worth a bit.

What surprised me most was that during my few months in the palace kitchens I met several people doing the sort of work I was doing who had done prison time, but I don't think they ever caused any trouble. They were very nice, in fact, and very pleased just to have a job. The nicest of the bunch was a man who had served twenty years for murder! None of us was ever vetted or asked questions about our past.

Seating, who sat where and why, was also intimately tied up with status, and a gentleman usher was traditionally in charge of making sure that the most important guests at a royal banquet were seated closest to the monarch and in order of rank. In that respect, nothing has changed. In the past, a mistake at a banquet could have serious consequences – a nobleman seated too far from the monarch might walk out, for example, or start a fight.

Handling food was strictly codified too – servers and carvers in the early modern period were to touch their own food with their left hands, but other people's food could only be touched with the right hand.

The elaborate ceremony surrounding food is perhaps best summed up by Paul Hentzner, a German lawyer who recorded in great detail an account of a three-year journey through Europe at the end of the seventeenth century. His travels included a visit to the English court. Hentzner's book was published in Latin in 1612 and later translated into English by Robert Bentley. Here is his oft-quoted account of dinner at the court of Elizabeth I:

> A gentleman entered the room bearing a rod, and along with him another who had a tablecloth, which after they had both kneeled three times, with the utmost veneration, he spread upon the table, and after kneeling again, they both retired.
>
> Then came two others, one with the rod again, the other with a salt cellar, a plate and bread; when they had kneeled, as the other had done, and placed what was brought upon the table, they too retired with the same ceremonies performed by the first. At last came an unmarried lady (we were told she was a countess) and along with her a married one, bearing a tasting-knife; the former was dressed in white silk, who when she had prostrated herself

three times, in the most graceful manner approached the table and rubbed the plates with bread and salt, with as much awe as if the Queen had been present. When they had waited there a little while, the Yeomen of the Guard entered, bare-headed, clothed in scarlet, with a golden rose upon their backs, bringing in at each turn a course of twenty-four dishes, served in plate most of it gilt; these dishes were received by a gentleman in the same order they were brought, and placed upon the table, while the lady-taster gave to each of the guard a mouthful to eat, of the particular dish he brought, for fear of any poison.

During the time that this guard, which consists of the tallest and stoutest men that can be found in all England, being carefully selected for this service, were bringing dinner, twelve trumpets and two kettle-drums made the hall ring for half an hour together. At the end of this ceremonial, a number of unmarried ladies appeared, who with particular solemnity lifted the meat off the table and conveyed it to the Queen's inner and more private chamber, where, after she had chosen for herself, the rest goes to the ladies of the court.

The Queen dines and sups alone with very few attendance; and it is very seldom that anybody, foreigner or native, is admitted at that time and then only at the intercession of somebody in power.

Leap forward several centuries and little had changed, beyond the food tasters checking for poison. Food as status symbol was central to Queen Victoria's sense of her own importance as queen. French food was all the rage and she employed highly expensive chefs and apprentice chefs trained in French cuisine, one of whom, Gabriel Tschumi, wrote a book about his experiences at Buckingham Palace.

Tschumi recalls the enormously elaborate meals demanded by the queen and the shocking waste she tolerated and at times encouraged. Vast meals of pheasant, grouse and wild salmon brought at great expense from Scotland were regularly thrown away because Victoria thought they were not up to the mark. And in tandem with her expensive French cook, Victoria kept a small team of Indian cooks who prepared food every day just in case anyone wanted to eat it. Very few – other than Victoria herself – ever did, so it was usually thrown away. But Victoria insisted several Indian dishes should be cooked every day anyway.

Conspicuous consumption and extravagance in everything reminded Victoria herself and everyone with whom she came into contact that she was queen. She also hated to abolish long-outmoded traditions. She continued for many years to pay her private musicians with a pint of wine a day in addition to their salaries.

Victoria's biographer A. N. Wilson reminds us that for much of her life Victoria drank only champagne. He also explains how 'she would eat enormous amounts – bacon and eggs for breakfast and sometimes porridge as well which she drowned in thick cream. She might have five or six courses for dinner and in old age became obsessed with Indian food, lots of curries and then plum puddings and cream tarts.'

Inevitably, Victoria became obese, as did her son Edward VII. Nothing could persuade her to eat less.

The pressure to produce food that would please the monarch

and the sheer difficulty of organising large numbers of staff meant the royal kitchens were often a scene of chaos where tempers regularly frayed.

There were always squabbles and shouting matches, but things became far more serious when, in 1841, Queen Victoria's head chef Charles Francatelli was arrested for fighting with the deputy comptroller of the household. The latter official, who was something of a grand figure, assumed, to his cost, that a lowly chef could be spoken to as if he were a kitchen maid. Francatelli thought of himself as an artist and took exception to this with his fists.

Agnes Cooke, interviewed in the 1980s when her memoirs were published, remembered her grandmother's stories from the Buckingham Palace kitchens, and her stories remind us that until well into the twentieth century little had changed in the daily routine below stairs.

My grandmother worked in the kitchens at Buckingham Palace from about 1905. She told me that the head chef was an absolute tyrant who would throw things at the maids if they made a mistake or were too slow to work. Very little had been modernised by then – the ranges on which the food was cooked were huge and the heat in the kitchen terrible. I remember Granny saying how she couldn't believe how much had to be cooked, especially for a banquet. She said maids would be peeling vegetables till their hands were red raw. Meals very rarely consisted of only one kind of meat – even breakfast included at least three different meats as well as eggs and fish.

Granny said the kitchen staff were never treated kindly – there was an idea that being soft with the staff would make them lazy.

In *The Private Life of the Queen* by 'One of her Majesty's Servants', published in the 1890s and then quickly suppressed, the anonymous author explains how the two solid silver dinner services at Windsor, with more than 1,000 pieces in total, were so heavy that the assistants employed in the kitchen were chosen for the work based on their size and strength – they had to be strong enough to carry stacks of heavy plates. The solid gold service, also at Windsor, was even heavier.

Interviewed by the present author in the 1980s, a former royal maid who worked at Windsor in the 1920s said:

I was always astonished that we were allowed to handle all the valuable dishes and plates used at Windsor – priceless things were occasionally dropped and broken and I'm certain things were regularly stolen, but not much was done about it.

You cannot imagine the bustle and rush in the royal kitchens at Windsor and Buckingham Palace, especially Buckingham Palace on the day of a big banquet. It would be weeks in the preparation. Imagine the head chef trying to control a kitchen filled with kitchen maids rushing here and there with utensils and bowls and dishes, ingredients, hot water, cold water, vinegar, salt, everything you can imagine. And it had to be done at speed or each course couldn't be served for everyone at roughly the same time and with the food still hot enough.

Then there were the maids who washed up. That, if anything, was even more fraught:

We just had ordinary soap in the early days to get the grease off hundreds of plates and knives and forks. We also used spirits – I mean alcohol – to do it, but there was no modern washing-up liquid. Then the silver cutlery had to be greased before it was put away or it would tarnish. Imagine that – every piece of silver had to be greased and there were hundreds of pieces, thousands even.

Many of the pans were never cleaned – they were what we called seasoned and in fact you were in trouble if you tried to scour an old pan. The head chef believed that a seasoned pan produced wonderful food while a new pan or a well-scoured pan produced food that tasted of metal, so you needed your wits about you not to make a mistake.

For a while we had a patent cutlery cleaner – it looked like a wooden butter churn. You put all the knives in the slots and then turned a handle and whirling brushes inside the wooden tub took the grease off and polished everything. But you had to be careful not to turn the handle impatiently – do it too fast and you might break the cutlery. The abrasive dust which we added to the cleaning machine was also applied by hand – it was really just a sort of brick dust. I used to think how odd it would be if the royal family knew they were eating with knives and forks cleaned in this very odd way – I mean with brick dust.

Edward VII inherited his mother's obsession with food. Indeed, his biographer Jane Ridley describes how he ate 'like a man possessed', scarcely chewing his food in his eagerness to get it down.

But food at the end of the nineteenth century, even for the royals, had changed. Roasted swan had long gone by this time and the royal family was enjoying the novelty of actually helping themselves from a sideboard at breakfast each morning, although a typical breakfast would still consist of vast quantities of eggs, fish, bacon, chicken, omelettes, kidneys, kedgeree, pork and lamb chops.

Like Victoria and Edward VII, George V employed a French chef, Henri Cédard. Though French morals were suspect in England, having a French chef was a sign of status, as indeed was the ability to speak French. George V, who hated travel, would have loved to stay permanently at Sandringham with his stamp collection; his chef was instructed so far as possible to cook only meat, vegetables and fruit that had been grown on the royal estates at Windsor, Balmoral and Sandringham. Despite his French chef, George wanted his food plain and simple. This was partly the result of his determination to seem as middle class as possible and thereby avoid the fate of other European monarchies overthrown in the years after the Great War, but it was also a reaction to his father's obsession with rich, elaborately cooked food, just as living quietly at Sandringham with his wife and children was a reaction to his father's opulent, irresponsible ways.

When Princess Elizabeth (as she then was) married in 1947, what could have been more natural than that the guests should eat the wedding breakfast from solid gold plates? And at Buckingham Palace in Elizabeth's time the number of staff working in the kitchens was positively medieval; they were able to serve dinner for up to 600 guests in Buckingham Palace's extraordinary 37-metre-long ballroom.

In the twenty-first century, the royal family no longer refer to all their servants as, well, servants. They are staff who are provided with sick pay, holiday pay and in some cases gym memberships and – most of the time – treated with kindness. The royal family must be a considerate employer as well as adhering strictly to employment law, but that doesn't mean senior royals have lowered their standards and are prepared to do without servants in any aspect of their lives.

And a few ghostly remnants of ancient food-related rituals were still in place towards the end of Elizabeth II's reign. The piper charged with playing below Elizabeth's window at Balmoral before breakfast each day, for example, was not that different perhaps from the trumpeters who heralded the arrival of her ancestors in the dining hall 600 years earlier.

Rather like Marie Antoinette playing at being a shepherdess at Petit Trianon, senior royals do occasionally try their hands at cooking – but just for the fun of it. Elizabeth II famously enjoyed washing up after family picnics at Balmoral. Her husband Prince Philip did the cooking, while she insisted on clearing up and cleaning the plates and cutlery. On one occasion, she noticed that the portable table on which she liked to stack the plates was coming apart. She asked for a screwdriver and tried to fix the table herself. She was apparently heard to murmur, 'Mmm, this is far more difficult than being Queen!'

Like her father and grandfather, Elizabeth preferred simple

food to the elaborate dishes served at banquets for heads of state and other political visitors. And she was perhaps happiest of all when quietly sitting down to enjoy the small jam circles she ate every afternoon into her late middle age with her oldest friend and former nanny, Bobo MacDonald.

Chapter Ten

Bedroom antics

'Do answer. You never know, it might be someone important.'
– Queen Elizabeth II, to a young woman
whose phone rang at a reception

'Whereas the voice of memory is universal and uncontested,
that of history is polyphonic and open to debate.'
– Arno Mayer, *The Observer*

The aristocratic staff in the royal household always have lives of their own outside the royal family. Ladies in waiting are no longer forbidden to marry and they work, if that is the right word, as ladies in waiting for only a few weeks each year. Under Queen Victoria, ladies in waiting were paid as much as ten times the annual pay of a working man for a relatively short period of service each year, but under Elizabeth II ladies in waiting were not paid at all.

The situation is comparable with the aristocratic men who for centuries have served as equerries and other senior staff; their role was and is to provide advice but also, perhaps more importantly, to provide suitably aristocratic companionship.

Equerries are paid today, but because they have traditionally been selected from the military, the Ministry of Defence foots the bill. In the financial year that ended in the spring of 2024, the cost of equerries supplied to the senior royals was more than £500,000, according to a Freedom of Information request submitted by the *Daily Mail* newspaper.

Despite many aspects of royal servant life reflecting the changed values of the modern world, the situation with equerries is decidedly un-modern. Until very recently, equerries were traditionally drawn from the 'best' regiments – such as the Blues and Royals and the Life Guards that only very rarely accept officers who do not have a gentry or aristocratic background. This policy was updated in 2014, but it will take some time for the change to be reflected in the makeup of the Household Cavalry. The fact that the policy existed for so long speaks volumes about the ancient idea that jobs with the royal family that involve day-to-day contact with monarchs and princes can only be offered to those who are just a little below the royals on the social scale.

A former Kensington Palace footman said:

No one mentions class divisions at the palace, but they are everywhere. All the equerries have cut glass accents and are privately educated; all the kitchen staff and domestics are state school educated and don't have the sort of accents the royals feel comfortable with. One senior royal who I don't want to name once casually remarked that equerries need to be good-looking and that working-class men never really have the right sort of looks for the job. She has her own equerries, as do all the senior royals, but I don't think anyone would argue with the statement that equerries don't really have anything to do. It's not a job. It's a tradition.

Aristocratic equerries feel less intimidated and perhaps also less dazzled by their proximity to royalty and few leave royal service after their stint with any great sense of loss. Lower down the social scale, one or two individuals among the male staff become far more devoted to the royal family than even the most enthusiastic equerry.

One man who matched even Bobo MacDonald in loyalty and tenacity was William Tallon, the Queen Mother's adored Page of the Backstairs. Tallon spent fifty years as servant, lunch companion, entertainer and confidant to a woman who once said to him, 'William, we are so lucky to live in an age when we can talk to each other – my father and grandfather would not have allowed me to exchange more than two words with a servant and I think that was very wrong.'

William took this as a compliment because he knew, better perhaps than anyone, how much the world had changed since he had been born into a working-class home in County Durham a few years after the end of the Great Depression. William became well known in his own right because of his sheer flamboyance and his immense gift for friendship – the parties he hosted in his little grace and favour gatehouse in the Mall, just a few hundred yards from Buckingham Palace, were legendary. William's life has been chronicled in a full-length biography by the present author, but suffice to say he is typical of those few servants, and even fewer male servants, whose devotion to the royal family becomes the dominant factor in their lives.

William's level of devotion is only matched by female servants in earlier centuries.

When Elizabeth I contracted smallpox in 1562, Lady Mary Sidney (née Lady Dudley), lady in waiting and mother of the poet Sir Philip Sidney, nursed the stricken queen. Smallpox was not always fatal. For every 100 people who contracted the disease, somewhere between five and thirty died, but those who survived almost always suffered permanent facial scarring. This was a serious matter in an era in which women, perhaps especially well-born women, were judged almost solely on their appearance. Lady Mary caught smallpox from Elizabeth and, according to one story, was asked to retire from the court because her disfigured face reminded Elizabeth of her own scars. Other versions of the story insist that Mary chose to leave the court and retire to her country house because she knew that, with her looks gone, she had lost one of the main reasons she had been there in the first place. Yet another story insists that Lady Mary wanted to leave, despite Elizabeth asking her to stay, because she knew nothing ugly was welcome at court.

Certainly, Mary's husband was unsympathetic. Like most senior courtiers at the time, he lived away from home for much of the time and when he saw his wife after her illness he wrote, 'I left her a full fair lady ... and when I returned, I found her as foul a lady as the smallpox could make her.'

Other royal servants became so devoted to a particular royal that they refused to work for any other – Anne of Cleves's ladies in waiting all refused to work for her successor, Catherine Howard, for example, choosing instead to stay with Anne after her divorce.

But devotion to the royal family is not always rewarded, as William Tallon, a modern equivalent to Mary Sidney, discovered after the death of the Queen Mother. Within weeks of her funeral, William was ousted from his job and his home, his more than fifty years' service seemingly of no account.

* * *

Among the most interesting intimate royal servants from earlier periods is Blanche Parry. Parry came from gentry stock rather than the aristocracy, but she had aristocratic connections – she was related to the Earls of Pembroke, for example. She seems to have been taken to court initially by her aunt Lady Troy, but connections were important here because Lady Troy, governess and Lady Mistress to Elizabeth I and her half-brother Edward VI, wanted someone she could trust to assist her.

Elizabeth was born in 1533 when Blanche, born probably in 1507, was already in her twenties, but having arrived at court she looked after Elizabeth almost from her birth until she, Blanche, died in 1590. Blanche's tomb in the village church in her home village of Bacton, Herefordshire, contains her monument: a statue of her and the queen she served for so long.

The inscription reads:

> Whyllste that my mystres lyvde
> In woman's state whose cradle sawe I rocket
> Her servant then as when
> Shee her crowne attcheeved
> And so remaend tyll death

It is easy to imagine that Lady Troy would have suggested her niece as an ideal person to serve at court – it was a classic example of one member of a family using their influence to get a position for a relative at court.

Blanche seems never to have put a foot wrong and in her more than six-decade career she rose to become one of Elizabeth's closest friends. Her great advantage over other women at court was not her birth status – she was, after all, only distantly related to the aristocracy – it was the fact that she had looked after Elizabeth when Elizabeth was a child. She took the place effectively of Elizabeth's executed mother Anne Boleyn. The ties made in childhood are often the hardest to break. We need only compare Blanche with Bobo MacDonald who (as we have seen and will see in more detail in a moment) in the 1920s began work looking after the princesses Elizabeth, later Elizabeth II, and her sister Margaret when they were in their infancy and she was aged just seventeen. Exactly like Blanche Parry, Bobo MacDonald never married and never left the woman to whom she devoted her life.

Blanche spent almost all her adult life with Elizabeth I and indeed along with Kat Ashley, she was one of Elizabeth I's most trusted intimate attendants. The epitome, in fact, of later servants who became indispensable to their employer.

Blanche was a fluent Welsh speaker and her most recent biographer, Ruth Richardson, argues convincingly, in *Mistress Blanche*, that Elizabeth would have sung lullabies to the baby Elizabeth (and almost certainly in Welsh) and that in later life the pair would use Welsh words to disguise their discussions about courtiers and conspirators. This shared intimacy can only have bound the two women ever more closely together. Richardson believes Blanche even accompanied Elizabeth to the Tower during a period of her life when she was in real danger of being executed on the orders of her sister, Mary.

Blanche had succeeded Kat Ashley on the latter's death in 1565 and was quickly promoted – she was made chief Gentlewoman of the Privy Chamber and was responsible for looking after Elizabeth's jewellery, in addition to much of the queen's most valuable clothes, her books and even her linen.

Elizabeth, like all monarchs in the early modern period, feared assassination, and she must have felt that anyone who had looked after her when she was a baby was probably someone she could trust as an adult.

Blanche was also careful never to overreach – she certainly used her influence with the queen to help her friends, but she never attempted unduly to influence Elizabeth. Better still, she never married.

Other gentry servants and ladies in waiting occasionally overreached themselves or interfered politically in the life of the court – this invariably infuriated Elizabeth and the guilty lady in waiting or woman of the bedchamber would either be physically assaulted or banished from court (occasionally both). In *Lust and*

Licence in Early Modern England, Johanna Rickman describes Elizabeth as being 'liberal in her use of blows'.

Blanche seems to have had an unusual ability to tread a line between helping her friends and family while remaining on good terms with her mistress. And the rewards for her loyalty were considerable: she was gifted land in Wales and Herefordshire as well as clothing worth a small fortune – most famously, she was given a magnificent dress that at some point in its history was repurposed as an altar cloth at Blanche's home church in Herefordshire.

For centuries, the origins of the Bacton altar cloth had been forgotten, but in the early twentieth century research by the then vicar of Bacton Church, Charles Brothers, suggested that the cloth had once been the major part of a magnificent and very valuable royal dress given to Blanche. More recent research has confirmed this. The silk cloth woven with silver thread, which would have cost a fortune to make, is still in the church at Bacton; it is now believed to be the only surviving dress once owned by Elizabeth I.

Like Blanche, Kat Ashley was trusted implicitly because she too had worked for Elizabeth when the princess's position was unsure – as a toddler Elizabeth had been removed from the succession by her father – and at times even dangerous.

Kat Ashley, née Champernowne, was born in or around 1502. Her origins are not easy to discover (her father may have been one of several Champernownes at court), but she was certainly aristocratic, perhaps more so than Blanche Parry. Kat became Elizabeth's gentlewoman in waiting in 1536. The following year, she seems to have become Elizabeth's governess. Many years later, Elizabeth acknowledged the enormous influence Kat had had on her. In addition to teaching her French and Italian, Kat apparently knew enough geography and even mathematics to give her mistress a good grounding in these subjects, but her story demonstrates both the benefits and risks of royal service.

When Elizabeth's father Henry VIII died in 1547, the various aristocrats who had surrounded the king began to manoeuvre to gain control of the nine-year-old Edward VI; others began scheming to marry either Elizabeth or her half-sister, Mary.

Thomas Seymour, who was the brother of Henry VIII's third wife Jane Seymour, took soundings to see if he might be allowed to marry Elizabeth. It was made clear to him that this was not going to be permitted, so instead Seymour married Catherine Parr, Henry VIII's widow. Bearing in mind Henry had been dead only a few months by the time the marriage took place, this would have caused murmurings, but when Catherine died in childbirth, Seymour began paying court again to Elizabeth; it even began to be rumoured that he had engaged in some sort of sexual activity with Elizabeth in her bedroom during his marriage to Catherine. Jealous of his brother's position as Lord Protector of the child king Edward VI, Thomas was in the meantime plotting to oust his brother and take control of the young king himself. The final straw came when he was discovered outside the king's bedroom at Hampton Court with a loaded pistol. Suspicions about his earlier behaviour with the young princess Elizabeth only added to the general conviction that his scheming was treasonous, and he was condemned to death in 1549. Kat Ashley was implicated, largely a result of Seymour's rumoured flirtation with the young Elizabeth, and as a result she was imprisoned in the Tower.

She might have told her interrogators that Elizabeth had not been particularly robust in her rejection of Seymour's flirting – this would have been extremely dangerous for Elizabeth – but she did not and this secured the future queen's trust. Kat was released from prison, but it was a narrow escape for both her and Elizabeth and the story reveals how even powerful women had a sense that less powerful men might still try to control them.

During Kat Ashley's imprisonment, it was Blanche Parry who took over in the Princess Elizabeth's private chambers, and when Kat died in 1565, Blanche was promoted. She continued to work for Elizabeth until her own death in 1590, by which time Elizabeth was fifty-six.

Four centuries later, when royal service was less obviously dangerous, the most enigmatic of modern royal servants was born in 1904.

Margaret MacDonald was born in a tiny cottage in the Black Isle north of Inverness. She left school at fourteen and began work as a maid in a local hotel. When she was still in her early twenties, she applied for a job as nursemaid to the Duke and Duchess of York, who, though very grand, were not in the direct line of succession to the throne. It was the Duke of York's brother who would later become Edward VIII – until his shock abdication propelled Margaret's new employers into the royal limelight and made their daughter Elizabeth heir to the throne.

Margaret started work in the Yorks' nursery soon after Elizabeth was born in 1926, which is probably why she was always closer to Elizabeth than to Margaret, born in 1930.

Margaret and Elizabeth were always well suited because, in many respects, both were completely uneducated. Elizabeth, it is true, enjoyed the privilege of French tutors, but acquiring French was seen as a social accomplishment rather than an intellectual one; it was an important means by which the royal family and the aristocracy were able to distinguish themselves from the lower orders. And it had a further advantage, as a former Buckingham Palace maid recalled:

> If they didn't want the footmen and the maids to know what they were talking about, they would switch to French. I thought it was very rude until I was told by a very senior member of staff that whatever the royal family said to a servant, it could not count as rude!

Elizabeth's relationship with Margaret MacDonald began when the princess was so young she would hardly have been aware of anything, but as she grew, she would have realised that she had a great deal in common with the girl from the Black Isle. They shared a love of the countryside and a dislike of modern ideas and intellectualism. This was important for Elizabeth because the royals have always been what, for want of a better word, can only be described as philistines. Elizabeth's father was once bellowed at by *his* father George V for browsing through a book of poetry. George V was convinced that any man who read poetry must be homosexual. Prince Philip had similar worries about his son Prince Charles, who was seen as far too keen on nature and art.

This strain of anti-intellectualism has long been characteristic of the royal family and it explains, in part at least, why the royals always feel more comfortable with their aristocratic friends (who can be relied on to hunt, shoot and fish) and their working-class employees who have not been tainted by a university education. It's the middle classes, especially of the intellectual kind, who are untrustworthy, and they are untrustworthy because the royal family has traditionally had nothing to do with them.

Margaret MacDonald, the daughter of a railwayman, was supremely trustworthy. She was one of a number of servants tasked with looking after Elizabeth and Margaret at the Yorks' Scottish castle, their home in Bruton Street, Mayfair, and their castle in Hertfordshire. As well as Margaret the nurserymaid, there were a nursery footman, a governess and of course a nanny, the formidable Clara Cooper Knight, known as Allah.

The legend that Margaret MacDonald got her nickname via a game she loved to play with Elizabeth is almost certainly true. A retired servant who worked at Bruton Street in the 1930s told the present author, during an interview in the 1980s, that the close relationship between the young Margaret and the princesses was obvious to all.

They were almost never apart and even back then in the early 1930s we knew that Bobo and Elizabeth had played a game constantly in which the two would hide from each other and then when one or the other was found they would shout, 'Boo! Boo!' This transformed slowly until the children gave up calling Margaret by her name and used her new nickname – Booboo or Bobo

– all the time, as children are wont to do. Elizabeth and her sister were much closer to Bobo than they ever were to their mother.

[The Queen Mother] was always a kindly presence, but like almost all great families of the time, she had nothing at all to do with the day-to-day care of her children. The governess and later on Bobo would present the children to their parents perhaps once a day for half an hour before being whisked off back to the nursery.

You can imagine as a child you begin to notice the world around you and like all young animals, we make our strongest attachments to the people who look after us – Elizabeth was sort of imprinted on Bobo and vice versa and it lasted the rest of their lives together.

Though she would never have admitted it, Bobo saw Elizabeth and Margaret as her own children – and in a sense, they *were* hers. Aristocratic families thought it was enough to be a parent on paper. They saw nothing of value in the actual business of cleaning and feeding and reading stories to their small children, or spending time with them: 'That was all farmed out to others – paid staff like Bobo – which is why, I'm sorry to say, so many aristocrats and indeed members of the royal family grew up to be a bit unhinged.'

A retired maid who worked at Buckingham Palace in the 1970s recalled Bobo in her middle and later years:

She was almost a ghostly presence in the palace by the time I knew her. I think the habit of being careful what she said had become so ingrained that she always seemed very restrained, very quiet. She had no life at all outside royal circles for more than sixty years. She didn't go home to a husband or even to her own home – she lived always in the palace and never far from Elizabeth. She even accompanied Elizabeth on her honeymoon!

She was always talked about in awestruck tones – even the aristocratic courtiers were in awe of her because they knew that if they upset her in any way, Elizabeth would make sure their jobs at the palace came quickly to an end.

Bobo ran her bath and just talked to her and you can imagine that with their history going back to Elizabeth's infancy, they could say anything to each other. After all, Bobo was the only person outside the family itself who was allowed to call Elizabeth by her nickname, Lilibet.

Elizabeth never felt comfortable if she was parted from Bobo for long, because in reality they were as close as two people could possibly be. I think Elizabeth found the idea of losing Bobo unbearable. When Bobo became quite frail in her last decade or so, Elizabeth prepared a suite of rooms at Buckingham Palace very close to her own rooms, and refused to allow Bobo to do any work at all. Bobo was rather put out by this, as she had loved her work and hated to be idle, but the Queen insisted because she was terrified that Bobo might die.

For her last years, Bobo was given the sort of treatment by staff and by the royals in general that only a family member would normally expect – but then Bobo *was* family. When Bobo died in 1993 at the age of eighty-nine, the Queen was distraught. In fact, it was said that she was never quite the same again; she became quieter and more formal even with her closest aides and friends. And she insisted that Bobo's memorial service should be held at the Queen's Chapel next to St James's Palace.

It is said that Queen Elizabeth II was the last of the great monarchs with a deep link to the ancient traditions of monarchy, and that is certainly true; but Bobo MacDonald also has her place in this tradition. She was almost certainly the last of the great royal servants.

Chapter Eleven

Ladies in waiting

—————————————

'Look, I'm not a bloody quiz show you know,
just here to answer questions.'
– PRINCESS MARGARET TO THE AUTHOR

'According to Princess Margaret, "You can't possibly
have a picnic without your butler."'
– ANNE GLENCONNER, *LADY IN WAITING*

Below-stairs staff in the royal household have only very rarely lost their lives as a result of their work. Courtiers, with their aristocratic connections and backgrounds, their sense of their own importance, were not always so lucky – Queen Elizabeth II may have been great friends with the Earl Marshal, the Duke of Norfolk, for example, but her ancestor Elizabeth I had the 4th Duke of Norfolk executed for stepping out of line.

With their power to order executions gone, today's royal family still occasionally take things into their own hands. When the comedian and actor Stephen Fry met Princess Margaret at a party and told her that he was descended from John Fry, a parliamentarian who had signed Charles I's death warrant in 1649, Margaret's response was to pick up a fork and stab him in the leg with it.

'There,' she said, as he yelped from the pain, 'We've got some of our own back.'

Historically speaking, queens would not have demeaned themselves by taking a fork to a recalcitrant lady in waiting, but they occasionally had them executed. Lady Rochford, one of Catherine Howard's ladies in waiting, was beheaded for allegedly helping her mistress meet her lover. More sceptical historians might argue that Catherine's husband, Henry VIII, rarely worried about the truth or otherwise of an accusation when he wanted to kill one of his wives and adding a 'guilty' lady-in waiting was a useful way of ensuring that Catherine's 'treachery' was less open to question.

But even if they didn't lose their lives, ladies in waiting and other aristocratic female servants were almost invariably caught between loyalty to their queen and loyalty to their husbands, who were not above using their wives to try to influence the monarch or even to spy on her.

This was one reason why Elizabeth I preferred her ladies in waiting to be unmarried, while accepting that, according to the standards of the time, it was generally agreed that it was a woman's duty to marry. But if they married without permission, they might be permanently banished from court, as the Earl of Essex's sister Dorothy found when she married Sir Thomas Perrot without the consent of the queen. Even a great favourite such as Lettice Knollys was banished after marrying without permission, but she was so badly missed that Elizabeth eventually forgave her.

Lady in waiting Bridget Manners, another great favourite of Elizabeth I's, who married secretly in 1594, was sent to prison by Elizabeth. But Elizabeth found once again that she couldn't do without her and she too was recalled.

Behind Elizabeth's attempts to control the lives of her ladies in waiting was both a sharp sense of politics and a keen sense of personal resentment. As Elizabeth was well aware, marriage meant that her ladies in waiting would become mouthpieces for their husbands, who would use them to exert power over the queen, and the ladies in waiting would not have the power to say no. But in addition, Elizabeth knew that she herself could never marry if she wished to retain the power she enjoyed as queen. So pure jealousy was central to her objections – if she couldn't marry for the sake of the kingdom then her ladies in waiting should not marry either.

Even in the private social sphere – if any part of a Tudor monarch's life can be described as private – power corrupted those who wielded it, and it has always corrupted both queens and kings, who have tended to bully and belittle their staff as well as doting on them.

In some ways even monarchs were subject to the unwritten laws of the system. A queen was not always free to choose her ladies in waiting or indeed any of her female staff. Catherine of Aragon could hardly have refused to accept the Duke of Buckingham's three sisters as ladies in waiting, as they were direct descendants of Edward IV. She was offered their services and was obliged to accept.

Centuries later, something similar was still happening – in 1839, Queen Victoria was told by Prime Minister Sir Robert Peel that her ladies in waiting would need to change from women whose husbands were known Whigs to women whose husbands were known Tories. Victoria refused the request – as monarch, she was in a stronger position than Catherine of Aragon – and as a result Peel declined to form a new government. That the appointment of ladies in waiting should have had such political significance as recently as the nineteenth century is extraordinary.

Ladies in waiting were always used as pawns by powerful factions – even the most aristocratic lady in waiting might struggle to resist the pressures of a male courtier, even if he was not related to her or not quite her social equal.

A queen might also be destroyed by an ambitious courtier and scheming female attendants. Alison Sim's *Masters and Servants in Tudor England* reminds us of the story of courtier John Lassells. Lassells wrote to Thomas Cranmer hinting at Catherine Howard's infidelity in order to curry favour with one of the most powerful men in the country. Henry wanted to execute Catherine Howard and he wanted Cranmer to find the evidence to enable him to do so; Lassells was happy to supply it.

Despite numerous biographers repeating the story that Catherine was certainly guilty of adultery, there is actually very little evidence to back this up, as Conor Byrne points out in his 2019 book *Katherine Howard: Henry VIII's Slandered Queen*. Byrne argues that it was Catherine's failure to tell the increasingly paranoid (and probably impotent) Henry of her previous romantic attachments (which were probably not sexual) that led to her downfall and execution. Once Henry had decided someone was guilty, finding evidence was a mere formality, but for the sake of outward show some hard evidence had to be found. When John Lassells helped find that evidence, his position at court was assured and the Lassells family have been closely linked to the royals ever since.

In more recent times, the role of lady in waiting has changed, but perhaps not quite as much as some might imagine. Soon after the 2023 coronation of Charles III, Queen Camilla announced her decision to abolish the role of lady in waiting and replace it with a new role – that of companion. Royal observers suspect that the name has changed but the role will remain the same. Camilla, like her predecessors, will choose as her companions exactly the same sort of aristocratic women who were formerly employed as ladies in waiting. In a sense, changing the name of the ladies in waiting is a belated recognition of their actual role – they are too grand to be staff, to be 'in waiting' (they are not expected to collect Camilla's dirty washing or vacuum her bedroom), but they are expected to entertain, give advice and act as paid companions; to be, as it were, professional friends from the same social class.

Despite having nothing to do beyond advising and amusing, ladies in waiting were traditionally well paid. As late as the mid-nineteenth century, as Adrian Tinniswood points out in *Behind the Throne*, Queen Victoria's ladies in waiting were paid

£500 a year (£60,000 in 2024) for doing nothing beyond staying within shouting distance of the queen for six weeks each summer.

But payment for female attendants at whatever level was always rather random and subject to whim: *The Lisle Letters* reveal that during Henry VIII's reign, maids of honour were paid £10 a year. During Elizabeth I's reign that increased to £40 a year. Maids of honour were a cut above ladies of the privy chamber, who were paid £34 a year.

On top of this were gifts – and gifts could be very valuable indeed. In Tudor England, a silk dress – a prerequisite for a lady in waiting – might cost £10 to make at a time when a farm labourer would earn perhaps £8 for a year's work.

The phrase 'clothes maketh the man' was key to status in the early modern period and indeed right up to the 1960s, when casual clothes began to destroy many more obvious class differences – differences based on whether one could afford a custom-made suit or resorted to cheaper, ready-made clothes.

Men had an advantage at court in earlier centuries: they were usually supplied with livery, while ladies in waiting and other female staff paid for their own clothes, unless they were lucky enough to receive clothing gifts from the monarch.

Ladies in waiting tended to be treated rather better than ladies of the bedchamber and indeed better than maids of honour, who were junior ladies in waiting. Always of noble birth, maids of honour had little to do beyond amusing the monarch and learning the ropes. Ladies in waiting were usually married (Elizabeth I's disapproval of her ladies marrying was unusual), whereas maids of honour were unmarried (by definition – they were maids, i.e. virgins) and young, perhaps just fifteen or sixteen. An official known as the Mother of the Maids was appointed to look after them (and their morals!).

Maids of honour were strictly treated – they were not permitted to sit down or fold their arms or speak if they had not been spoken to and their main duty was to stand like 'delicate orchids in china vases', as former servant Rose Plummer put it in an interview with the author. 'They were human decorations!'

Why were they not allowed to move or speak? The answer is that it 'showed the monarch could govern even a person's desire to scratch their nose'.

But as they were little more than children, they could still get into trouble – and frequently did.

In her exhaustive study *Ladies in Waiting*, Anne Somerset describes how chaotic the lives of maids of honour and ladies in waiting could be. At Windsor in the sixteenth century, for example, the maids of honour were made to share a room. That was not uncommon – in fact, most people shared not just a room with others but also a bed – but the problem was that the servants kept peeking in at them; eventually they asked for a partition to be made to free them from prying eyes.

An extraordinary anecdote described in William Thoms's 1839 book *Anecdotes and Traditions, Illustrative of Early English History and Literature* (and quoted by Anne Somerset) shows the remarkable lengths to which one man went to make disruptive maids behave:

The Lord Knolls, in Queen Elizabeth's time, had his lodgings at

Court, where some of the Ladyes and Maydes of Honour us'd to friske and hey about in the next roome, to his extreame disquiete a nights, though he had often warned them of it; at last he gets one to bold their owne backe doore, when they were all in one night at their revels, stripps off his shirt, and with a payre of spectacles on his nose and Aretine [his penis] in his hand, comes marching in at a posteren doore of his own chamber, reading very gravely, full upon the faces of them. Now let the reader judge what a sadd spectacle and pittifull fright these poore creatures endur'd.

Early accounts of courtly life, especially when taken from diaries of the time, record sometimes intense jealousies and backbiting. By contrast, modern accounts such as Anne Glenconner's *Lady in Waiting*, published in 2020, tell us rather less. They tend to emphasise how wonderful and kind everyone is, especially when anything has to do with the late Queen Elizabeth II. Glenconner describes Elizabeth always as ravishing, always calm and serene. And Margaret is always a delight. The real interest of Glenconner's book – which is very interesting indeed – is its revelation that many aristocrats who have worked for the royal family are actually completely mad.

She also reveals that as late as the 1950s everyone she knew (with the possible exception of her husband, Colin Tennant) belonged to the same narrow social set. Her husband was never quite allowed to forget that in the early nineteenth century the Tennants had made their money as grubby industrialists who invented bleach. Anne Glenconner grew up on her family's vast estate at Holkham in Norfolk, the ancestral seat of her father, the Hon. Thomas Coke, later Earl of Leicester. Lord Coke (pro-nounced 'Cook') lived exactly as his ancestors in the eighteenth century had lived, with teams of indoor and outdoor servants and no grubby links to trade (or bleach). The young Anne spent her summers at a castle in Scotland and was a regular playmate of the princesses Elizabeth and Margaret. She grew up to be debutante of the year, a maid of honour at Elizabeth II's corona-tion and then lady in waiting to Princess Margaret.

It was a life in which status was conferred by the accident of birth and by doing no practical or menial work at all (as Lady Glenconner is the first to admit). Being a maid of honour and then lady in waiting was simply to be a paid (latterly unpaid) companion, and in that sense the twentieth-century lady in waiting was identical to the Tudor or Stuart lady in waiting.

Lady Glenconner insists that Princess Margaret was a great friend, but the evidence for this is only convincing if we assume that great friends are often very unpleasant to each other.

One of Princess Margaret's maids, the modern equivalent to a Tudor gentlewoman of the bedchamber, in an interview with the present author, said:

Margaret was occasionally very nice to her maids but was often horrible, but she was horrible because she was unhappy. She would sometimes give you a dressing-down in front of any number of people if you had just placed an ashtray in the wrong place; she might even pick it up and drop it on the floor, leaving ash everywhere, which I then had to pick up. Sometimes she apologised for this sort of thing, but not always. She could also be rude to her ladies in waiting and maids of honour if she found them irritating – sometimes because all they did was try to keep her amused. They never contradicted her or argued because she had to be right. And she didn't like good-looking maids!

I remember when she was sent a new young, very pretty maid. The maid was polite and very good at her job, but a day or two after she started work, Margaret asked for her to be moved elsewhere because she thought Lord Snowdon [her husband] would try to sleep with her. I heard her say on the telephone, 'Tony will be pawing that poor girl five minutes after he sets eyes on her. Thank God she isn't a handsome young man, because that would just speed things up – the girl might last five minutes, but a boy I'd give two minutes.'

Maids and maids of honour were always vulnerable to sexual predators such as Lord Snowdon, although maids more so than maids of honour, who were used to giving rather than receiving orders.

The ancient equivalent to the modern maid was the chamber-er. These were the women who did the real work around a queen; the maids of honour might take messages or wind an occasional watch, but they didn't get their hands dirty, and ladies in waiting were considered too important even for watch winding.

In the twenty-first century, maids work shifts and they have some sort of life outside the palace walls. In former times, they were expected to be on call virtually twenty-four hours a day and seven days a week, as Nancy Jackman recalled:

Right up to the Second World War, after which it got difficult to find servants, maids were given one day off a week, sometimes just one afternoon – and the royals, like all those who employed domestics, expected us to be grateful. We all knew the ladies in waiting, who did absolutely nothing but talk to the queen and her sister and try to amuse her, and it never occurred to us to wonder why they never helped with the jobs we did. But that was the way of the world then and I suppose we just accepted it.

*   *   *

'When manpower was cheap, maids and servants generally were everywhere,' as one former royal servant explained to the present author. But that was especially the case at Whitehall, the vast sprawling palace that extended from present-day Westminster Abbey almost to Trafalgar Square. Whitehall was a hotbed of intrigue in which maids of honour and ladies in waiting were caught up continually in the struggle for position and influence.

When Whitehall burned down in 1698, change was inevitable because the king, William III, insisted on moving to the much smaller and quieter palace at Kensington; almost overnight the swirl of intrigue became much less intense. Pressure on living quarters at the new palace was such that maids of honour were forced to live ten minutes' walk from the palace in Kensington Square and domestic staff, especially kitchen staff, began to be recruited locally.

Kensington also played host over the following century to

three queens: Mary, Anne and finally Victoria. Female monarchs caused what were perceived as huge difficulties politically and socially – the proprieties meant they had to have female staff and companions, but their political advisers were still all male, and there was always a conflict between the male sense that women were inherently inferior and the practical and political reality that a woman was head of state and, in former times at least, the most powerful individual in the country.

As recently as the reign of Elizabeth II, Prince Philip complained that he was the only man in the country who did not have the traditional male right to give his children his surname. The Queen eventually gave in to his complaints and added the name Mountbatten to the family name, Windsor.

In the nineteenth century, Prince Albert, Victoria's consort, felt equally aggrieved that he could not rule his wife. He raged at Victoria for not allowing him more say in the running of the country, despite knowing this was constitutionally impossible. His view was that even if she happened to be queen and ruler of Britain, he was, by right of sex, ruler of her.

Despite her loathing of the whole idea of women's rights (she hated the idea of votes for women), Victoria resolutely refused to let Albert interfere in her constitutional role. Instead, she compromised by persuading Parliament to agree that if she were incapacitated in any way, he should rule as regent.

The dangers from male ego were more starkly apparent in Elizabethan England. We know the Earl of Essex eventually refused to accept Elizabeth's authority, partly because she had made him an indulged favourite. This seems to have convinced him she was weak, ill-advised and in need of a firm male hand. Essex decided her male advisers were not up to the job and that he should remove them. Elizabeth was female and therefore less able than a noble earl such as Essex to choose wisely. Elizabeth refused to bow to Essex's attempt to usurp her power and he was executed.

Scheming against the monarch was a constant danger, but it was always particularly acute when a woman sat on the throne. Much of this scheming would be channelled through a monarch's ladies in waiting, as we have seen, but, being aristocrats, ladies in waiting were also often ruthless schemers in their own right.

When Anne Boleyn fell pregnant again in late 1535, she must have hoped her position was assured, but she miscarried her son in January 1536 and the court began to move against her. She was hated by many for what was seen as her overweening ambition. A member of the powerful Howard family, which included the Duke of Norfolk, she had been a lady in waiting to Catherine of Aragon, whom she famously supplanted, but she was widely regarded as arrogant, unpleasant and unsuitable, a woman who as lady in waiting had plotted to steal the queen's husband. Anne's recent biographer Hayley Nolan argues that her subject was a far more sympathetic character than we have been led to believe, and there is no doubt some truth in this, but few doubt that she had schemed to become queen. After her miscarriage, she found other well-born women were now scheming against her, chief among them another lady in waiting, the Marchioness of Exeter.

The end result of the plots against Anne was that she was

supplanted by the more pliable Jane Seymour, who was perceived by her grand ladies in waiting, especially the Marchioness of Exeter, as less difficult and less troublesome. Jane was famously sweet natured by contrast to the fiery Anne Boleyn.

Some years later, the marchioness herself was implicated in a plot against the king. The Exeter Conspiracy led to the execution of the marchioness's husband, Henry, Marquess of Exeter. The marchioness narrowly avoided execution and after the death of Henry VIII and his son Edward VI, she became lady in waiting to Queen Mary.

Scheming at one level or another was typical of the lives of ladies in waiting throughout the early modern period, and as Anne Boleyn discovered, it could lead to disaster.

Elizabeth I, as we have seen, kept a tight hold on her ladies in waiting, but her successor, James I of England and VI of Scotland, who was far more interested in his male attendants than in his wife's ladies in waiting, tended to let them do as they pleased while making sure they were very well rewarded. As Anne Somerset points out in her study of ladies in waiting, James was if anything overly generous, giving, for example, his wife's first Lady of the Bedchamber Jane Drummond the enormous sum of £2,000 in 1605 – worth more than £500,000 today. Lady Walsingham was given the same sum in 1616 and even the Mother of the Maids was gifted £100 (£25,000 today). By paying his wife's ladies in waiting these generous sums, James was of course helping to ensure their loyalty. Few others, even among his noblemen, were likely to match his generosity.

Charles II was equally generous to his wife's ladies in waiting and other female members of staff, but this was often done to placate them after they had been seduced – or seduced and then discarded in favour of a new lady in waiting. Charles's philandering created intense rivalries, as his mistresses often lived at court and competed for preferment and financial reward both for themselves and for their families and friends. This reached its apogee when Charles gifted one of his most magnificent palaces, Nonesuch in Surrey, to the Duchess of Cleveland, his mistress and his wife's Lady of the Bedchamber. Having obtained Nonesuch, the duchess had the house broken up and sold to pay her enormous gambling debts. As a lady in waiting, she had been foisted on Charles's queen, and the two women loathed each other.

Charles also ennobled his children by the duchess: the present-day Duke of Grafton and Duke of Cleveland are descended from Cleveland's illegitimate children. One lady in waiting's role as mistress to a king has ensured at least two aristocratic families are among Britain's wealthiest in the twenty-first century.

As the seventeenth century ended and the eighteenth wore on, the monarch and the wider royal family, though no longer able to exert absolute political power, which had shifted to Parliament following the execution of Charles I, was increasingly the focus of social ambition. Just as ladies in waiting had once jostled for position, for money and for power, so they continued to compete for those benefits conferred by proximity to the monarch.

The merry-go-round on which the already wealthy and influential became more so by association with the monarch intensified – Queen Anne's lady in waiting Sarah Churchill, for example, was a dominant if latterly domineering royal companion. When Anne offered Sarah's husband John Churchill a dukedom, Sarah turned it down on her husband's behalf and only agreed he would accept it when Anne had been persuaded to add an annual pension of £5,000 for life from Parliament, along with £2,000 a year from the privy purse.

What taxpayers thought of this is not recorded.

Anne and Sarah eventually fell out and from 1711 until Anne's death in 1714 they were completely estranged – but by then Sarah had secured the dukedom for the family, as well as the vast palace at Blenheim, Oxford, that the family still enjoys today.

For a century and more after the death of Queen Anne, the Hanoverian kings tended to try to enrich themselves rather than their senior staff, whether ladies in waiting or gentleman attendants. George I had accepted the throne of England largely because he needed to improve the fortunes of a family that governed a small and not especially wealthy German principality. The feeling that the British should pay handsomely for the four Georges who succeeded each other ran deep, and it reached a peak of greed when the numerous sons of George III only agreed to discard their mistresses and take wives in return for large grants of taxpayers' money.

Despite his sons siring more than twenty illegitimate children between them, it took until the Duke of Kent, fifth child of George III, to produce a legitimate heir who survived long enough to inherit the throne. This was, of course, Queen Victoria, who collected staff, whether ladies in waiting, doctors or coal heavers, the way some people collect teapots.

Over the course of her long reign, Victoria employed more than thirty-seven ladies in waiting and ladies of the bedchamber; countless maids of honour were also in attendance. All these women were titled and it is fascinating how many of them were related to aristocratic attendants from earlier centuries – Lady Emily Villiers, for example, was descended from Sir Edward Villiers, Master of the Mint, whose half-brother George was a favourite of James I, while Lady Anne Spencer-Churchill was descended from Queen Anne's favourite Sarah, Duchess of Marlborough.

To avoid the sordid idea that ladies in waiting were paid staff, they were often given what was described as a retainer, and from the mid-nineteenth century up to and including the reign of Elizabeth II, ladies in waiting rotated – serving a fortnight or a few weeks at a time at most. Kitchen maids might work all year round, but the old idea that aristocratic roles must not look like work endures.

Elizabeth II's ladies in waiting were not paid even a retainer, but it would be hard to find a single lady in waiting in recent times who was not wealthy in her own right. Centuries of royal service, adultery and scheming have ensured that most of those families from which ladies in waiting are usually drawn are now rich enough to work for nothing.

Ladies in waiting dislike the idea that theirs is a job and they have been keen to maintain their distance, literally and metaphorically, from paid staff, but during the reign of Elizabeth II something dramatic changed: treating below-stairs staff as inferior became increasingly unacceptable and even the most aristocratic lady in waiting is far more likely than not to try to treat people with modern ideas of egalitarianism in mind. As a retired Buckingham Palace maid recalled, 'Oh, it was as if we all became human overnight! Instead of looking down their noses and telling us to fetch and carry without looking at us, we were suddenly being asked if we would mind awfully doing so and so.'

But the old ways die hard and even towards the end of her reign Elizabeth II would have been astonished had anyone questioned the fact that all her friends and ladies in waiting, whether paid or unpaid, were invariably rich and titled.

In that respect at least, little has changed in five centuries – Queen Elizabeth still had her Mistress of the Robes and her Page of the Backstairs, her first and second footmen, her stewards and gillies. In her last decades, Elizabeth II had between ten and twelve ladies in waiting; all elderly, all aristocrats and all known to the Queen through family connections or family recommendations.

The difficulties for ladies in waiting in the modern world are illustrated by the career of Lady Susan Hussey. Lady Hussey, daughter of the 12th Earl Waldegrave and employed as a lady of the household from as early as 1960, got into trouble for appearing to assume that someone who was black must originate from somewhere outside the United Kingdom. Lady Hussey, whose friends insist she is not by any means a racist, simply thought she was making innocent small talk, but as the product of an all but vanished age – she was born in 1939 – she was not entirely in tune with 21st-century sensibilities.

Other ladies in waiting of recent times have been decidedly eccentric, as Agnes Cooke recalled:

Well, there was a lady in waiting who was very friendly with Philip's mother, Princess Alice of Battenberg, when Alice was living at Buckingham Palace, and they used to smoke cigarettes together in Alice's apartment – so much so that they regularly set fire to it. And despite being very grand indeed – a member of one of Britain's oldest and most aristocratic families – this particular lady in waiting used to wander about with a cigarette stuck behind her ear, like a coal miner or a carpenter.

All the officials were terrified she would go for a walk or go out with the Queen one day with the cigarette still there. But they were terrified to ask her not to do it, as she was quick-tempered.

Another very elderly lady in waiting to the Queen Mother became very dotty in the end and she used to accuse the male staff of all sorts of odd things. She once complained that one of the pages had put his foot through her bedroom window one morning and trodden on her finger!

The era of ladies in waiting came to an end when King Charles III and Queen Camilla came to the throne in 2022. Or did it? Camilla, as we have seen, announced that she would have 'companions' rather than ladies in waiting, but many have seen this as a simple rebranding exercise to avoid accusations of elitism. So, who are these companions? Well, they include the Marchioness of Lansdowne; Baroness Chisholm, daughter of the 1st Baron

Egremont; Lady Katharine Brooke; and Lady Sarah Keswick. In addition, there are Mrs von Westenholz and Mrs Troughton. So, have we reached a more egalitarian era? Hardly – Mrs von Westonholz is married to a baron and Mrs Troughton is the King's second cousin.

When it comes to ladies in waiting, as with so much to do with the royal family, everything changes and nothing changes.

Chapter Twelve

Lords a-leaping (and no Jews or Catholics allowed)

'History in the royal family isn't just one damned thing after another. It's more just one damned Old Etonian after another.'
– BUCKINGHAM PALACE STAFFER, AUTHOR INTERVIEW

'They'd never admit it, but what they really want is a return to the good old days when they could cut people's heads off.'
– RETIRED KENSINGTON PALACE MAID, AUTHOR INTERVIEW

Courtiers don't traditionally get to choose for whom they work. They might – now as in the past – be dismissed simply because a monarch dies or they fall out of favour, but in the vast majority of cases courtiers hang on to their positions with grim determination. And new masters can present hilarious challenges. As the historian Lucy Jago reminds us, when James I took the English throne after the death of Elizabeth I, the courtiers who immediately began to curry favour with the new monarch found themselves faced with a special difficulty: they began to write frantically to each other complaining that they could not understand a word the new king said because he had such a strong Scottish accent.

Few aristocratic advisers, courtiers or otherwise, would go as far as Lord Altrincham when in 1957 he publicly criticised Queen Elizabeth II for surrounding herself with old tweedy, Etonian aristocratic advisers – and was publicly slapped in the face for his cheek. Altrincham's criticisms actually did shift things a little and there has been a gradual and very reluctant tilt towards a more egalitarian approach to the appointment of courtiers.

As Valentine Low points out in his book *Courtiers*, the arrival of Ed Perkins as an assistant press secretary in the royal household in 2007 was an astonishing break with tradition. Ed Perkins's may have been a relatively lowly courtier appointment, but this was a revolution nonetheless. Why? Because Perkins had attended a comprehensive school.

But if Ed Perkins was a long time coming, it took far longer – until 2024, in fact – for the first female equerry to be appointed. Captain Kat Anderson was given the job in February 2024 and will accompany King Charles III on official engagements.

For the purposes of this book, I've taken courtiers to mean male equivalents of ladies in waiting. In many ways, the term 'courtier' might be said to be almost meaningless in the twenty-first century since, arguably, the royal family's staff are all simply employees, no different from the kitchen maids, chefs and footmen. Yet, after all, there *is* still a difference and one might argue that Ed Perkins is merely a token gesture; in the world of the courtier, the old class system is still alive and hard at work.

It is certainly true that there have been non-aristocratic courtiers in the past, but these non-aristocrats always seem to be from the gentry class, people who attended Marlborough rather than, say, Eton, and were descended from local knights and squires rather than from dukes and earls.

Alan 'Tommy' Lascelles, who famously played a part in preventing Princess Margaret from marrying Peter Townsend, was just such a man. The son of a Royal Navy commander, his years as a courtier encompassed four reigns – George V, Edward VIII, George VI and Elizabeth II – and though he may seem to break the mould as he was not himself an aristocrat, he was Lord Harewood's first cousin and Harewood was married to Edward VIII's sister, Princess Mary.

Like many middle-class royal servants, Lascelles was deeply conservative. He loathed the idea that a divorced middle-class man – Peter Townsend – should even think of marrying a senior royal, yet when he heard that Edward VIII's friend Fruity Metcalfe had left his wallet containing letters from the then prince in a brothel, he passed it off as a 'boys will be boys' joke. In his eyes, aristocratic boys were just different.

From a historical perspective, the really fascinating courtiers are those aristocratic individuals whose appearance at court was always based far more on who they were connected with than who they were: what makes them so interesting is that for much of the time they had to walk a dangerously thin line between their role as friends and near equals to the monarch and their role as employees who could be dismissed from court in an instant if they proved unsatisfactory in any way.

As the centuries passed, courtiers from the highest levels of the aristocracy were increasingly unlikely to be dismissed, as the monarch's power was never threatened by their presence – because the monarch had actually lost almost all his or her political power anyway. Attendant lords were no longer told to raise armies from among their serfs. Instead, they provided companionship and advice and in return were often given sinecures that made them rich.

Of course, the gravy train was also intergenerational. Aristocrats hovering around the royal family passed their roles as courtiers on to their sons, often for generation after generation. The Cecils, for example – courtiers since the time of Elizabeth I – and the Dukes of Norfolk and Northumberland. And despite the fact that a Duke of Norfolk was executed in 1572 for treason, the Norfolks have mostly been on the best of terms with the royal family. The current Duke of Norfolk is a descendant of Edward I, as is King Charles III. The two families' histories are inextricably interwoven.

Indeed, so close are they that the Norfolks might claim with some justice that they once had as much right to the throne as anyone – certainly their right was at least as good as that of, for example, William of Normandy or Henry VII.

Power struggles and raising armies are both now things of the past and, as the Earl Marshal, the Duke of Norfolk presides quietly over his vast estate and organises royal funerals, for which he is unpaid. On the other hand, he would be the first to concede that his £100 million, 46,000-acre fortune has been accrued largely through his royal connections.

A preference for the aristocracy is hardwired into the royal family because they have been linked together for millennia. There is still a sense that they are fundamentally different from the rest of us. It is rather like the situation with cricket – until recently, games were regularly played between what were known as gentlemen and what were known as players. This baffling distinction was understood by everyone until well into the twentieth century. The gentlemen were so called because they were not paid to play. That is what made them gentlemen. The players, by contrast, were paid and so were by definition not gentlemen.

Members of the royal family and their aristocratic servants still behave as if life at court were an old-fashioned game of cricket. They cannot generally be expected to clean their own houses or travel by bus; they cannot be expected to live without staff or to educate their children with the bulk of the rest of society.

In this respect, aristocratic courtiers, like monarchs, live today much as their ancestors lived at court in Tudor and earlier times. And deference to the aristocracy is not, as many people imagine, simply part of traditional ceremonies and no longer part of people's everyday lives. In fact, the opposite is true. The present author once visited Blenheim Palace on a wintry day in the 1990s. The then Duke of Marlborough arrived at the house in a chauffeur-driven car which pulled up at a side entrance to the palace. No one was around, not a single member of the public for half a mile in any direction, and yet, rather than simply open the car door himself, the duke waited for a member of staff to come out of the palace to do it for him. And who can forget the huge fuss when, in 2018 and while still a working royal, Meghan Markle closed a car door by herself.

* * *

It is a curious fact that gentlemen servants and courtiers were once known as henchmen, a word defined by the Oxford English Dictionary as 'archaic – a squire or page, a right-hand man, a political follower whose support is chiefly for personal advantage'.

But even henchmen need rules, or at least they did. In a poem written around 1460 and reprinted by the Early English Text Society in 1868, an anonymous poet provided the following advice for courtiers working for the royal family:

> In his [the monarch's] face lovely ye look,
> Foot and hand ye keep full style [still],
> Fro clawing and trypping, hit is skille
> Fro spettynge and snetynge [nose blowing] kepe ye also.
>
> Be privy of vaudance [breaking wind] and lette hit goe,
> And loke ye be wyse and felle [serious]
> And thereto also that ye governe ye well
> Into ye halle when thou dost wende.

In the early modern period, aristocratic and gentry staff (not to mention the lowlier kitchen staff) probably needed this sort of basic advice, because few people had anything resembling modern ideas about cleanliness and the need for privacy when dealing with one's bodily functions. Everyone from kitchen staff to the very grand would urinate wherever they happened to be – the corners of chimneys were favourite places.

The Eltham Ordinances of 1526, perhaps the first attempt to codify the rules of the court, were drawn up by Cardinal Wolsey, ostensibly to reduce the number and cost of courtiers and servants but also, in Wolsey's words, to remove 'rascals and vagabonds now spread and remaining and being in all the court'.

In reality, the ordinances were designed to consolidate power in Wolsey's hands and to remove power from those members of the privy council who did not see eye to eye with the cardinal. It was a shrewd move: once written down, the rules had an objective reality and few realised there might be a difference between rules and Cardinal Wolsey's rules.

The battle for influence between Wolsey, something of an outsider, and the king's other closest advisers in the privy council – his courtiers – reflects almost exactly a difficulty that has plagued the English court up to the present day. Henry VIII's privy council consisted entirely of nobles, many of whom had known the king since they were children; they felt their advice to the king should be paramount and the advice of lesser men, however able, should count for less. In other words, the talented commoner (Wolsey) must always defer to the frequently less talented but well-born attendants.

Talented advisers are taken more seriously in the twenty-first century – which is why the senior royals employ communications teams – but the old guard, the courtiers drawn from the aristocracy, still exert a powerful influence at court. Just as the nobles at Henry VIII's court tended to look down on men like Wolsey, so too even today there is a tendency among Charles III's aristocratic courtiers to conflict with professional advisers whose backgrounds are usually very different from their own.

Of course, the primary aim of noble and less well-born advisers then and now is the exercise of power and the pursuit of money. Many of today's noble families who are related to the royal family or have worked as courtiers for them for generations turned their wealth into prodigy houses, vast buildings built far more for show than for comfort. The Cecils, for instance, provided generations of royal advisers. William Cecil, later Lord Burghley, one of Elizabeth I's closest advisers, built his imposing pile, Burghley House near Stamford in Lincolnshire, while his son Robert Cecil, 1st Earl of Salisbury, built Hatfield Hall in Hertfordshire. These houses, and others like them, survive today and still reflect the power of the families who own them. Aristocratic courtiers were usually able to retain their wealth and influence down the centuries. Wolsey, whose father was probably a butcher, overreached himself; he turned a country house at Hampton Court into a vast mansion but famously failed to ensure Henry VIII's marriage to Catherine of Aragon was annulled. Despite his undoubted skills as a courtier, Wolsey lost his head – and it was far easier for Henry to execute Wolsey for his failure than it would have been to execute a more aristocratic courtier, because Wolsey was widely considered an upstart.

History has portrayed Wolsey as a ruthless manipulator, but whatever his faults, he was remarkably good at inspiring loyalty in those who worked for him. Thomas Bellot, for example, worked for Wolsey for more than forty years; George Cavendish, who likewise worked for Wolsey for years, refused an offer of employment with Henry VIII after Wolsey's execution.

The days when courtiers might die for failing to do the monarch's bidding are long gone, but in Tudor England pressure on Queen Elizabeth from aristocratic courtiers who thought they knew better than she did was continual. We have seen how the Earl of Essex was executed after trying to remove Elizabeth's advisers, but Essex was not alone.

In *Masters and Servants in Tudor England*, Alison Sim explains how Elizabeth I instructed her gentleman usher Simon Bowyer not to allow anyone into her privy chamber if they did not have the right to be there. The Earl of Leicester, far grander than Bowyer and one of the queen's favourites, told one of his friends that all he would have to do to gain admittance to the queen's privy chamber was to mention Leicester's name. When Leicester's friend presented himself at the door, he was turned away by Bowyer. Leicester was furious and there was a real risk Bowyer would be assaulted or even killed. Elizabeth backed Bowyer against Leicester, but the outcome might easily have been very different – as a much more modern story from Agnes Cooke illustrates.

Reflecting on the tussle for precedence among aristocratic staff in the twentieth century, Agnes recalled:

Everyone was very sensitive about their status in the palace. The very grand courtiers behaved more arrogantly than the Queen herself. They swept in and out issuing commands in cut-glass accents as if they were still running the navy or the whole of the British military. One of them, a cousin of the Queen, in fact, was kept waiting by a member of the admin staff and that poor person was asked to leave the very same day. But here's the strangest thing – the very same man had a reputation for being charming and polite to everyone, even the kitchen staff like us. But that was typical of royal service – it attracted people who could roar one minute and purr the next!

*   *   *

Dictionary definitions of the word 'courtier' vary, but not by much. Most agree that a courtier is someone who attends the court of a monarch, but a secondary meaning includes the idea that a courtier is someone who seeks favour in an ingratiating manner. All agree that courtiers have traditionally been drawn from the nobility. But the word has mostly been used, as we have seen, to distinguish between the noble or well-born servant and the kitchen maid.

One result of employing so many aristocrats and members of the gentry class is that the royal family has to put up with a large number of eccentrics. Members of the palace communications team tend to get very hot under the collar about this sort of accusation, but it is true, partly because the royal family, being eccentric themselves (and living decidedly eccentric lives by modern standards), are naturally attracted to eccentrics.

There also tends to be rather a lot of slavish deference (and ingratiating behaviour), because that is the way the royals like it.

And where there is slavish deference, there are petty jealousies. If one senior royal has twenty courtiers, all the senior royals want twenty courtiers – which is why, by 2012, Prince Charles (as he then was) employed 125 staff. Probably most of these people had some work to do, but many of them were employed simply to reassure Charles that he was doing a good job. Courtier numbers have always expanded to fill the space (and consume the funds) available. With large numbers of lightly employed courtiers at Buckingham Palace and Kensington Palace, each with their own agenda and loyalties, the royal household, the palaces and even the country houses of the royals become hotbeds of gossip and secret manoeuvring.

In his book *Behind the Throne*, Adrian Tinniswood reminds us that in the mid-nineteenth century there were eight lords in waiting who were paid a great deal simply for turning up occasionally. One of Queen Elizabeth II's courtiers had the unenviable and no doubt onerous job of handing the late Queen a £10 note for the collection whenever she attended church at Sandringham.

A Sandringham staffer interviewed by the present author explained that the equerries and other staff fought over the chance to present the £10 note – but one wonders why the Queen was unable to fish into her own handbag for the money.

The Queen went along with a lot of things because she felt they were traditional and I think she worried that she might be seen to be digging around in her handbag in an undignified way for the £10 note, so it was easier to make an arrangement with a member of staff. She said in my hearing, 'One has to deal with a great deal of nonsense.'

Tinniswood quotes an elderly courtier who explained the staffing system to the Prince of Wales, later Edward VIII. He said that to make things run well what was needed was 'a man and a half for every job'.

There are still far too many senior staff, equerries, private secretaries, assistant private secretaries, aides de camp, pages, footmen and so on, but it was far worse in the past. Tinniswood quotes the Liverpool Financial Services Association, which asked in 1856 if the queen really needed thirteen men to bring in the coal, or eleven members of staff to support the master of the household. Most damning of all, the association stated that 'the ladies of the bedchamber should be ashamed of themselves for accepting £500 a year for the honour of keeping the queen company for six weeks'.

A full-time maid at that time might be lucky to receive an annual wage of £50 and one week's holiday.

Gentlemen attendants, courtiers, were always paid more than women of any rank, and pay differentials based on sex and social standing have changed little in centuries. In Tudor England, for example, gentlemen of the privy chamber were paid £50 a year while grooms of the privy chamber received £20 a year. As ever, women were discriminated against – a maid of honour, we may recall, was paid just £10.

Courtiers often competed to ingratiate themselves with the monarch. Sir Bryan Godfrey-Faussett took up stamp collecting because his boss, George V, was a keen collector. Godfrey-Faussett's efforts were rewarded when in one year his salary was increased by more than 30 per cent and he was given grace and favour apartments (i.e. free accommodation) at Sandringham and Buckingham Palace. Godfrey-Faussett was a rather skilled courtier and thus avoided the mistake that befell another of George V's courtiers. Chatting to the king one morning, the courtier said, 'Did your royal highness hear, some damned fool yesterday paid £1,400 for a single stamp?'

The king replied, 'Yes, I was that damned fool.'

An amusing example of courtiers currying favour with the monarch came when Edward VII decided to have his trousers made with turn-ups. If anyone else had done this at the time, he would have been condemned as a vulgar cad, but because the king started this sartorial innovation, the cloud of courtiers surrounding him rushed off to their tailors to have their trousers altered to include turn-ups.

Perhaps because they rely on paid staff to do everything for them, members of the royal family seem to have been singularly unlucky in some appointments. One of Edward VII's nannies later murdered five of her children, and Colonel Russell Williams, who was Queen Elizabeth II's pilot during a temporary posting, later committed two murders.

By the turn of the twentieth century, domestic royal servants and other below-stairs staff were routinely signing confidentiality agreements when they began work for the royals, but well-born advisers and courtier-friends have not always been so encumbered. It was somehow assumed, as it always had been, that a gentleman servant could be relied on to be discreet without the need for any written guarantees. But mistakes still occur – there was uproar at Buckingham Palace, for example, when Martin Charteris (descended from the Earls of Wemyss and an Old Etonian) let slip to a journalist that Sarah Ferguson, later the Duchess of York, was in his view 'vulgar, vulgar, vulgar'.

One of the difficulties is that courtiers sometimes struggle to tell friend from foe. Until the 1990s, journalists were largely drawn from the lower or middle classes; they traditionally started working for the newspapers aged sixteen and worked their way up. Such journalists were easily singled out by upper-class royal staff as untrustworthy. Then, suddenly, journalism became fashionable and out went what one courtier called 'the dirty mac brigade' and in came privately educated newspaper journalists such as Old Etonian Geordie Greig, sometime editor of the *Daily Mail*. Greig is descended from generations of royal courtiers, and his twin sister Laura was lady in waiting to Diana, Princess of Wales. Suddenly all the old verities were gone.

*   *   *

Anyone who thinks courtiers are not a strange bunch of jealous manipulators need only read Valentine Low's detailed account of what he calls the hidden power behind the crown. His book, *Courtiers*, though fascinating, is almost too difficult to follow, such is the rate at which advisers come and go; one minute they are in favour, the next they are out, often because a newcomer whispers in the ear of the king or queen (or Prince of Wales) that old so-and-so is useless and should be got rid of in favour of the person doing the whispering.

Of course, there are exceptions, and commentators including Low marvel at the extraordinary fact that, occasionally, a courtier will last more than a decade – but the marvelling is all down to the fact that lasting this long is very rare.

Low's study and others like it show that courtier titles are largely meaningless: there is an endless stream of private secretaries, press secretaries, assistant press secretaries, deputy private secretaries all basically doing elements of the same job (remember the old rule – one and a half men per job). And then there is the comptroller of the household, and the Lord Chamberlain, who looks after the monarch's money (despite the title, this is not a political post).

To be a courtier is to be lost in a sea of confusing titles that reflect the confusion in the royal household itself. The problem is that the royal household tries to mix new ideas with a desperate longing for the past, when tradition and over-staffing were the norm.

King Charles III's laudable attempts to reduce the size of the royal juggernaut may involve reducing the number of working royals, but it does not apply to the number of courtiers and personal staff.

One member of the late Queen Elizabeth II's kitchen staff, interviewed by the present author, said of the courtiers, 'They are the biggest bunch of backstabbers you could possibly imagine – they all try continually to get the Queen and the Prince of Wales [now King Charles] to pay most attention to their advice so they can lord it over all the other courtiers.'

At times, courtiers even seem to feel they are superior to members of the royal family. Tommy Lascelles thought Edward VIII selfish, immoral and unfit to be king, and Edward VII's courtiers despised his womanising. Perhaps less justifiable was the senior advisers' dislike of Prince Philip when he was first seen as a possible match for Elizabeth. He was viewed as suspiciously Greek, vaguely impecunious and with an unsuitable family background – he might have been a prince, but he was poor and obscure, and his sisters were married to Nazis.

Elizabeth seems to have put her foot down and insisted on marrying Philip – no one has ever denied it was a love match – in the full face of objections from the ranks of aristocratic courtiers who believed their Victorian attitudes and values should not be questioned even by their royal employers.

One said, 'It's not the individual monarch who matters – it's the reputation of the institution itself.'

Michael Fawcett, who started his career as a royal footman, seems to have beaten all the aristocratic courtiers at their own game. The then Prince Charles was entranced by Fawcett's ideas and by his energy and drive, but the courtier grandees were baffled that they were always overruled in favour of someone they saw as something of an upstart.

In an interview with the present author, one very grand retired courtier said:

Fawcett had a kind of instinctive ability and I'm afraid it is true that we looked down on him because we had nothing in common with him and we didn't trust him. Officially he was the prince's valet, but in reality, he was really the courtier's courtier! Very close to the prince, his advice was taken almost unquestioningly. We were jealous, I'm afraid, of his closeness to the prince. We all had similar backgrounds, Eton and Oxford or Eton and one of the best regiments, and here was this former footman beating us at our own game. We didn't like it, but you have to take your hat off to old Fawcett. He was brilliant at the dark arts!

Fawcett, on whom Prince Charles relied for almost two decades, is one of the few exceptions that prove the rule: a brilliant courtier who was not from a grand or titled background. Queen Elizabeth, the Queen Mother, famously said of her page William Tallon that she could dispense with any of her other staff but she could never dispense with William. Charles said almost exactly the same thing about Michael Fawcett.

As with the Earl of Essex in an earlier era, Fawcett eventually overstepped the mark; having survived two scandals, he met his downfall in 2021 after becoming embroiled in a cash-for-honours investigation involving a donation to one of King Charles's charities.

King Charles has an oft-noted propensity to be dazzled by confident new courtiers – someone who insists all the advice he's been given up to that point is terrible will often meet with a warm reception. Charles always thinks, with some justification, that the new broom sweeps cleanest.

Certainly, new brooms among royal courtiers have led to significant changes. Charles's parents and grandparents relied on senior staff who disliked change and the modern world, staff who thought a monarch's role was formality in public and hunting, shooting and fishing the rest of the time. Charles has broken the mould, and courtiers in the past – even the recent past – would have been horrified.

A former member of Charles's staff says:

Charles has always combined what many of the old guard at the palace see as trendy lefty issues – the homeless, conservation and global warming, for example – with a love for the sort of die-hard right-wing pastimes that the old guard think he should stick to. I mean fox hunting, stalking in the Highlands and salmon fishing at Birkhall.

Charles is an animal lover, certainly, but that doesn't stop him being a keen supporter of field sports. He knows that stalking, for example, can involve shooting and only wounding a deer (which may then take some time to find and kill), but he would hate the sport to be banned. So, he mixes a modern sentimentality about animals, if that's what you want to call it, with a very medieval attitude to hunting and shooting.

Courtiers who survive in royal service for decades are rare in the twenty-first century. Failure to achieve the king's aims no longer leads to the executioner's block, but it often leads to dismissal:

Charles worries far more about how the public see him than his mother ever did and if he gets bad publicity, it can put him in a rage and make him turn to anyone who says they can help. His mother was always rather more easy-going, at least until something went badly wrong – then she could be the ice queen. She wouldn't box your ears, but if you were being iced out, you really knew it.

Beyond the exceptions, such as Michael Fawcett, is it really true that the bulk of courtiers in the modern era have been as grand as their counterparts centuries ago? Well, let's take a look.

Just a random sample will give a flavour of the thing. Sir Martin Gilliat, for many years Elizabeth II's private secretary, was educated at Eton and Sandhurst; Martin Charteris, also private secretary to Queen Elizabeth, was at Eton and Sandhurst; Jamie Lowther-Pinkerton, private secretary to the Duke and Duchess of Cambridge and to Prince Harry, attended Eton and Sandhurst; Michael Adeane, private secretary to Elizabeth II, and his son Edward Adeane, private secretary to Charles as the Prince of Wales, both studied at Eton and Cambridge. The Queen Mother's equerry Ralph Anstruther was also educated at Eton and Cambridge, while equerry Alastair Aird attended Eton and Sandhurst. In fact, the list is almost endless: Rupert Nevill, private secretary to Prince Philip: Eton and the Life Guards; Rupert Ponsonby, Elizabeth II's Master of the Horse: Eton and the Royal Wessex regiment; Robert Fellowes, formerly private secretary to Elizabeth II: Eton and the Scots Guards.

Baron Fellowes was probably closest to the ancient idea of the royal courtier, as he was married to the sister of the late Diana, Princess of Wales, as well as being a cousin of Sarah Ferguson. Elizabeth II was his godmother.

What this list shows is the extraordinarily narrow social

stratum from which senior royal servants are taken. Meritocracy has only washed at the edges of the work of the traditional courtier.

The atmosphere that swirls around 21st-century courtiers is at least as incestuous and claustrophobic as it was in the Tudor court and though ability is a factor, connections were and still are far more important.

The royal family are famously distrustful of intellectuals, but they like their advisers to be well educated and clever – hence the preponderance of Cambridge graduates. Even Ed Perkins went from his Welsh comprehensive school to Cambridge and one doubts very much if he would have made it to the palace without his Cambridge background.

Apart from being clever, the massed ranks of Old Etonians were also employed because they were already known by or related to the royal family.

One former member of staff says:

The royal family feel comfortable with people who are just one rank down from them and this has always been the case. People with regional accents and who went to secondary modern schools or comprehensive schools don't know anyone connected to the royal household, so they are not taken on in the main in jobs that are heard about on the grapevine rather than being advertised. Rupert Featherstonehaugh or whoever will recommend his friend or cousin, Davenport Hines, and Charles or Camilla will say, 'Yes, he's a good egg, solid and reliable,' and next minute they've got the job. If the government or a commercial company happened to be run like this, there would be uproar.

Part of the appeal is that the royals actually like the eccentricities of the well born – there have been equerries and private secretaries who shoot pigeons out of the windows of the palaces, others who practise their fly casting on the palace lawns and yet others who wander the corridors making strange noises. One very aristocratic member of the Buckingham Palace staff had to be asked not to wear a bow tie containing a flashing bulb that was turned on via a secret button in his coat pocket.

The past is littered with aristocratic courtiers who behaved badly or oddly. Perhaps the most famous and outrageous was John Wilmot, Earl of Rochester. Charles II loved Rochester for his outrageously entertaining behaviour. He once pretended to be a doctor, setting up his stall on Tower Hill and selling quack remedies. On another occasion he set up as a travelling repairer of pots and pans and then instead of repairing people's pots, he broke them – and was almost murdered by the crowd.

Charles thought Rochester's exploits amusing until Rochester wrote a clever poem mocking the king. He was banished from court – but quickly recalled because, like most monarchs, Charles was easily bored and Rochester was the perfect antidote to the overly serious court.

Members of the royal family are always more comfortable when they stick with what they know, but as their staffing decisions are increasingly in the public eye, they have had to move with the times a little – which is why Ed Perkins was able to join the royal household as an assistant press secretary in 2007. But that was a very rare event and noted for precisely that reason.

Other changes have been slower to come – domestic staff in the royal palaces have always been addressed by their surnames, for example, while senior household staff always address each other by their Christian names. Of course, this being the palace, there are always exceptions. The system is baffling to outsiders, as one member of the kitchen staff explained. 'It's completely mad – like all the ordinary staff, I mean the domestic staff, the footmen were traditionally addressed by their surnames, but with one exception: the nursery footman. For some reason now lost but dating back to Victoria's time, he is always addressed by his Christian name.'

Naturally, everyone across the various royal residences is polite now to everyone else – the upper-class staff know they have to be careful how they treat the maids and other kitchen staff – but there are limits to this new, egalitarian world. A maid at Kensington Palace interviewed by the present author said:

> The very grand members of staff are friendly to the domestic staff, but they are not going to invite us to tea or to marry their sons. But there is no point complaining about it – if you want to work here, you have to accept that that is the way it is.

No Jews or Catholics were employed by the royal family until the 1970s (the Duke of Norfolk being the exception that proved the rule), but gay staff were always welcome. The late Queen

Mother explained, 'If we don't employ these people, we will have to go self-service.' She believed that the great advantage of employing gay members of staff was that they were more likely than others to devote themselves wholly to royal service, since it was assumed in those days that they would have no family life outside the palace.

But gay staff at a senior level are rarer – a notable but fairly recent exception being Mark Bolland, known to William and Harry as Blackadder, after the Machiavellian television character. Prince Charles, as he was then, was deeply impressed by Bolland's modernising instincts: he was persuaded by Bolland to mix more with the Spice Girls and less with the Old Etonians. Bolland, if you like, was a latter-day Lord Altrincham.

* * *

I've called this chapter 'lords a leaping' because even if courtiers do not arrive at the palace with titles, they usually leave with them. This contrasts hugely with the situation with domestic and other staff lower down the scale – very few kitchen maids or cleaners, footmen or gillies receive titles or awards at the end of their service.

Even Bobo MacDonald, who, as we have seen, served Elizabeth II for the whole of her adult life, was only appointed a lieutenant of the Royal Victorian Order – until 1984 this represented the fourth grade of the order. Martin Charteris was appointed a Knight Grand Cross of the Royal Victorian Order, the highest grade, on his retirement, and he would have been deeply insulted to be appointed a lowly lieutenant of the order. The difference can be summed up in two words: social class. Margaret Mac-Donald was a railwayman's daughter; Martin Charteris was the son of Lord Elcho and had studied at Eton and Sandhurst.

Even the Queen Mother's favourite servant, Page of the Backstairs William Tallon, received an award appropriate to his lowly status. He was awarded the Royal Victorian Order Gold medal, which sounds like the highest award – in fact, it is the highest award but in the lowest class. The fine social distinctions embodied in the Royal Victorian Order, an order exclusively in the gift of the sovereign, precisely reflect the social distinctions of a vanished world to which the royal family still largely adheres.

Even the immensely skilled Michael Fawcett received only the lower Royal Victorian Order, while the Duke of Norfolk and various other hereditary peers were invariably appointed to the top ranks of the Victorian Order. Aristocratic courtiers receive grades of the Royal Victorian Order that entitle them to be referred to as knights or dames. The absurd result is that a string of already titled aristocrats are given additional titles – these include Lady Hussey, Dame Annabel Alice Hoyer Whitehead and the Marquess of Cholmondeley.

Field Marshal the Lord Guthrie of Craigiebank had perhaps the most wonderful reason for being appointed to the order: it was his reward for being Gold Stick in Waiting. No doubt an onerous appointment.

A former senior adviser to Prince Charles (as he then was) explained in an interview with the present author:

Courtiers are awarded the highest honours because that is the way it has always been done. If you are the son of a lord and you work as private secretary to a senior royal, you feel your family background entitles you to the highest awards the royals can bestow, and the king or queen wouldn't dream of offering you anything less. It's a question of rank and entitlement and I think the royals themselves don't feel brave enough to award the Victorian Order on merit alone because it would cause ructions among the very grand, with whom they mostly mix. But also, the royal family instinctively accept that the very grand honours go to the very grand.

I remember the suggestion – made as a joke – that one elderly courtier might be happy with the lowest Victorian order as he already had a hereditary title. The man left the room with a very stony look on his face. The senior staff, and I include myself in that, take themselves very seriously!

One of the more interesting things about entitled courtiers is that they are deeply intolerant of other people behaving as if they are entitled. When Meghan Markle, now the Duchess of Sussex, insisted on wearing a particular tiara for her wedding to Prince Harry, for example, it was the courtiers (who often feel more protective of the royal family than the members of that family themselves) who were up in arms. Harry was enraged when Meghan's request to be allowed to wear a particular tiara from Elizabeth II's collection was turned down by the Queen's staff. He no doubt believed that (as he famously put it), 'what

Meghan wants Meghan gets'. On this occasion it was not to be and Elizabeth herself intervened to explain gently and in person that, 'Meghan cannot have whatever she wants'. This was by no means the first time Elizabeth had supported a decision made by her staff in the face of tantrums from her children or grandchildren.

Had Meghan been an English aristocrat, the problem with the tiara (and much else besides) might not have arisen, as the old guard at the palace might have been more willing to accommodate an aristocrat's wishes.

The courtiers were almost as outraged when Meghan tried to hug a singularly stiff Old Etonian equerry. He flinched as if she'd tried to poke him in the eye, as one staffer put it.

Perhaps one of the most interesting changes in the modern world of the palace courtier is that where once the lower staff – the maids and chefs, the gardeners and cleaners – were overawed by the Old Etonians, they now often see them as figures of fun. Where once the lower classes were mocked for aping their betters – for trying to improve their diction or drop their regional accents – now the upper classes are sometimes mocked for their strangulated vowels, their pretentions and sense of entitlement. Anyone who listens to the late Queen Elizabeth's radio broadcasts in the 1950s and 1960s and compares them with broadcasts made thirty or forty years later will realise that even the Queen tried to tone down her extraordinary accent. As one former member of the Buckingham Palace staff put it, 'The Queen and all the family used to say "hend" instead of "hand", or "heve" instead of "have", but they don't any more, or at least not so much.'

One anecdote best sums up the real change in social values and attitudes. It was the late 1970s. Two very grand members of the Buckingham Palace staff were talking while a small group of maids were cleaning and tidying the room.

The first courtier, tall, thin, and very aristocratic, said, 'And how's your brother?'

The second, equally grand courtier, equally tall and thin, replied, 'He's fine, thanks.'

The first courtier said, 'What's he doing these days?'

The second replied (proudly), 'He's a Master of Hounds.'

The maids, despite their best efforts, collapsed into fits of giggles.

This would never have happened in the more distant past because below-stairs staff were so greatly in awe of the grandees. Laughing at them would have meant instant dismissal.

Courtiers who were close relatives of the royal family were not only immune from criticism; they were also difficult to discipline in any way.

When the singer Elton John and his songwriting partner Bernie Taupin were invited to a party attended by Elizabeth II, they found the Queen her usual self, but one or two of the aristocratic hangers on were less than dignified.

Taupin relates how in the middle of a conversation taking place just a few feet from the Queen, Lord Lichfield suddenly keeled over. A famously heavy drinker, the Earl of Lichfield had simply passed out. With barely a flicker of an eyebrow, the Queen said, 'Oh dear, Lichfield's gorn again...' and immediately through the nearest double doors came four bewigged footmen, who carried Lichfield out.

Chapter Thirteen

Modern times: Mystic Meg,
or England versus America

'Her compassion was floating on clouds of good fortune...'
– ALICE MUNRO

*'Oh God, Margaret, Andrew, Harry
– there's one in every generation.'*
– PALACE OFFICIAL TO THE AUTHOR

'Margaret really can't help it, you know.'
– QUEEN ELIZABETH II ON HER SISTER

The years since the accession of Elizabeth II in 1952 have seen more changes in the way the royal family treats and interacts with its staff than any other period in history – which is why this period perhaps deserves a closer, more forensic examination.

Above all else, the modern royal family is a celebrity family. The monarch's constitutional role is largely symbolic and their strangely eighteenth-century lifestyle – the palaces and carriages, the enormous wealth – are all underpinned, as we have seen, by vast teams of servants from every social class; servants who have their own lives and their own view of their employers.

For centuries we had only the royal family and the aristocracy to look up to, but by the 1960s we had all turned our attention to a new kind of celebrity – typified by the Beatles and an increasing number of cinema and television stars. Under pressure, then as now, to remain relevant, the royal family dramatically increased its support for charities and other good causes and, while clinging to its ancient privileges, made a point of working hard and being seen to work hard. It was as if attending several hundred events each year was payback for enjoying private lives of extraordinary luxury – luxury made possible by armies of servants.

The difficulties for the royal family in relation to the whole servant world are best exemplified by two women who found being royal extremely difficult: Princess Margaret and Meghan Markle.

Over the years since her death, I have spoken to a number of people who worked for Margaret and one theme emerges: having grown up in a world in which servants were seen almost as a necessary evil, she had lived into a more democratic age and, as one former maid put it, 'she could never really quite believe that she needed to change the way she treated her staff'.

Margaret's particular difficulty centred on the fact that the servants might notice how badly she got on with her husband: 'If they started a row when there were any servants around, she would almost run towards us shouting, "Shoo! Shoo!" and once I even remember her saying to one of the cleaners, "Go on, bugger off!"'

Margaret had a reputation for being extremely demanding and bad-tempered, but one or two of her former servants remember her kind side: 'When she heard I was getting divorced, she insisted I take extra time off if I needed it – she gave me two weeks and said if it wasn't enough, I was to take more. She was really sweet about it.'

At the other extreme she might be demanding and short-tempered.

She would suddenly turn into a nitpicking, obsessive person and do the sort of things she despised in others. For example, if she went out for the evening, as soon as she returned to Kensington Palace, she would rush across to her recently acquired television and feel along the top of it to see if it was still warm. If it was warm, that told her the servants had been watching her television, which would send her into a rage. She also hated it if any of her personal things had been moved without permission and would berate a servant in front of others, which could be humiliating. She didn't care because she had, I think, a slightly sadistic streak or maybe wanted to hurt people because she had been hurt.

Margaret's treatment of her staff has a transitional feel to it. She had a great deal of her ancestors' tendency to treat staff as objects, at the same time occasionally seeing and responding to their humanity. When she got angry with her staff, it was often because she was angry with her life and especially with her relationship with her husband, Lord Snowdon.

Snowdon had many lovers – of both sexes – during his marriage to the princess. He even slept with one of his mistresses the night before his wedding and it was later discovered that one of his girlfriends had given birth to his child during the early period of his marriage to Margaret.

Snowdon, a lawyer's son from north Wales, exemplified what the 1960s had done to society. In an earlier age, someone from his background would have found it impossible to marry into the royal family, as Princess Margaret continually reminded him during their bitterest rows. A former member of Margaret's staff said, 'Margaret would tell her husband that rather than marrying him, she should have offered him a job as her footman because at least he would have been good at that.'

Contrary to popular belief, Margaret, although surrounded by apparent friends, was actually very lonely:

I remember being with Margaret and discussing some trivial aspect of her week's schedule and she suddenly began to weep. It was very embarrassing at first, but then she suddenly began talking about how miserable she was and that all her so-called friends only wanted to be with her because she was a princess.

According to one of Princess Margaret's longest-serving members of staff, she actually had a long-term relationship – 'not quite an affair' – with one of her courtiers.

He was a very quiet, handsome man, but not quite from the top drawer by any means. Didn't look much like her old love Peter Townsend, but I always thought he had something of George VI [Princess Margaret's father] about him. I think that was the appeal. She was always kind to him and they spent a lot of time together when Lord Snowdon was absent – which was most of the time. It might have been a sexual relationship because Margaret was very highly sexed and he was a good-looking man who was very sympathetic, but I'm not sure we will ever know. But I often saw them having those sorts of conversations that only people who are very comfortable with each other tend to have.

One of the great difficulties in Princess Margaret's marriage was that she assumed that because she was a princess, Lord Snowdon, with his distinctly middle-class background, would always do as she wished him to do. She assumed that because he was lucky to have her, he would behave, but Snowdon – liberated as he saw it by the new freedoms of the 1960s and the contraceptive pill – was having none of it.

Although he liked the idea of having married a member of the royal family, he had no intention of changing the bachelor lifestyle he had enjoyed before his marriage. In fact, Snowdon used his celebrity status as Margaret's husband to seduce more women than he might otherwise have done.

A former servant remembers:

Margaret was often incensed that her staff – from her maids to her ladies in waiting – seemed to prefer Lord Snowdon, who was immensely charming and always very polite. Even her sister [Elizabeth II] made it obvious she liked Snowdon and found him less difficult than Margaret, but then he had all the benefits of being a member of the royal family and none of the drawbacks – he could leave Kensington Palace whenever he liked.

For Margaret, this was far more difficult and even her relationship with Roddy Llewellyn was fraught with difficulties: 'Margaret was really in love with Roddy Llewellyn, but she was class-obsessed and she worried her friends and senior members of her staff looked down on him, which they did.'

Feeling that both Roddy Lewellyn and her husband would have been servants in an earlier age left Margaret confused and sometimes bitter. And, almost inevitably, she took this out on her staff.

Her sister Elizabeth, who was far happier in her marriage and far more stoical about her husband's occasional infidelities, never took out her frustrations and anger on her staff – but then she was both a more balanced character than her sister and absolutely certain about her role in life.

Buckingham Palace staff almost universally recall how she always seemed to be 'cool, calm and collected':

She was classically good with servants: never over-familiar, but never unkind or dismissive. And she combined this with moments of great kindness – she famously gave one of the guards at the gate of Windsor Castle a bottle of water during an extremely hot summer when the poor man looked as if he was about to faint. She liked the guards, kitchen staff and gardeners at Windsor and Buckingham Palace – often I think she preferred them to the courtiers who advised her and sometimes irritated her.

Very few people know that if a member of Elizabeth's staff was struggling with a health issue and faced a long wait to be seen by the NHS, she would arrange and pay for private health care on their behalf.

King Charles and his brothers Andrew and Edward and sister Princess Anne have inherited a mix of their mother's 'cool kindness' with servants and their aunt Margaret's occasional explosive temper. One of Andrew's former servants said:

A bit like his aunt Margaret, Andrew always behaved as if he was frustrated about not being the first-born and therefore destined to become king. This frustration made him a bit of a bully in private, I think. If he liked a member of his staff, he could be very loyal and supportive, but he couldn't resist being imperious and bossy and bad-tempered if anything went wrong or wasn't done exactly to his liking … I think he felt it went with being a dignified and imposing member of the royal family, which is how he wanted to be seen. Some members of his staff, I won't say a majority, privately thought he was the classic school bully – just the sort of person who used to bully his brother Charles at Gordonstoun [Charles's school].

Several former servants recalled Andrew insisting on a member of staff being moved to other duties because he disliked a mole on the man's face. On another occasion Andrew is said to have arranged for a member of his staff to be moved because the man was wearing a nylon tie.

The temptations of personal power over staff can lead to surprising acts of ill temper. According to a now retired member of the Buckingham Palace staff, Prince Edward once tore a strip off his driver for looking too often in his rear-view mirror.

Rather than bullying his staff, King Charles either becomes convinced that the people who work for him, even the lowly domestic staff, absolutely adore him or he becomes paranoid that he can't trust them. Like his mother, he hates palace gossip reaching the newspapers – just as she did, he always uses black blotting paper so the servants can't read anything he's written and sell their stories to the newspapers. But he knows that his staff, and especially the senior aristocratic staff, will occasionally gossip to newspaper editors whatever he does to try to prevent it.

'It's inevitable,' said one former member of Charles's staff.

If they don't do it for money, they do it for fun over lunch at their clubs with an old schoolfriend. In the past, they would never have been friends with anyone as grubby as a journalist, but times have changed and some very grand people now work for the media and they all know each other – I mean the courtiers and the senior editors.

One member of staff believes that Charles's staff tolerated his occasional outbursts of irritation because 'everyone knows what a rotten childhood he had'. Some of his behaviour as an adult, especially towards his staff, was the sort of behaviour 'you'd expect from a toddler and Charles still occasionally behaved like that because when he was very young, he'd never been allowed to be a toddler!'

Camilla has long been seen as the mother Charles never had, but as well as being a calming influence when he loses his temper, she also gives Charles new perspectives on his role, new perspectives that he finds refreshing.

One member of staff explained that, at one point, Camilla hated the idea of being queen and would regularly say to Charles, 'Can't we get away from all this protocol – it's all bollocks.' Charles, who hates swearing, would demurely reply, 'You're doing it [becoming queen] for me, darling.'

The occasional tantrums of King Charles, the coolness of Elizabeth II and the bullying tactics of Prince Andrew have all been inherited in different measures by Prince William and Prince Harry. One of Harry's former servants says:

When most of the public think of Harry, they perhaps think of the sad-looking boy following his mother's coffin after her death in 1997. And many of Harry's problems do stem from that disaster in his early life, but people forget he is also his father's son. I remember once in his private apartments I'd muddled something – some of his papers on his desk or something. He was immediately angry and it was out of proportion to the problem, or at least I thought it was.

I was surprised at how cross he was about something so trivial, but his other staff had experienced similar incidents. We thought it was a bit rich complaining about me being muddled given that Harry was probably the most muddled of all the royals of his generation. The joke used to be that Harry was very much like the Prince Regent in the *Blackadder* television series. People used to say that without a servant, Harry would take two weeks to put his own trousers on.

Both Harry and William could be cruel about Camilla too. The boys' nicknames for her included Lady Macbeth, Cruella de Vil and the Witch of the West.

Several of Harry's former staff insist that his vulnerability gave him sensitivity and charm, but like his brother William and his father Charles, he was prone to flashes of irritation.

I don't really think they like the fact that they have to be polite most of the time these days, but they try their hardest. Interestingly, Harry became much more bad-tempered and pickier after he and Meghan started living together in Nottingham Cottage in 2017.

The problem was that she felt that he was too deferential both to his family and to the people who worked for them as a couple. She didn't like the fact that he tended to ask staff if they would mind tidying up or bringing something to him. With her American background she felt that when you pay people to do something you just issue commands and that Harry should just issue commands as she did.

A former member of the Kensington Palace communications team says:

I actually rather liked Meghan. She was very straightforward and matter of fact, but some people didn't like that because they felt she had got a bit above herself. Even the kitchen maids, I think, were a bit jealous, which made them very critical of Meghan. They liked Harry and felt very protective of him and then along comes this American woman who – they felt – made Harry into a less likeable character. But as one of Harry's own friends from the military said, Harry was a man waiting for a woman to mould him, and Meghan was that woman.

It's easy to forget that when Harry first started dating Meghan, both William and Kate found her delightful – 'they thought she was a breath of fresh air,' remembers one staffer.

A junior member of staff explained that in the early days when the Fab Four were still getting along, she once came across Meghan and William doing a jokey parody of 1950s jiving together. William was apparently very good at it.

But problems began to arise fairly early on. Tension developed between William and Harry as a result of Meghan's warm, friendly, hug-everyone approach. It made William uncomfortable because she hugged him virtually every time they bumped into each other; the hugging and cheek kissing fuelled gossip among the staff that Meghan was flirting with William, which she was obviously not, but the tense atmosphere caused by all the touchy-feeliness (and the resultant gossip) deepened the rift between the brothers.

Being a young king in waiting is rather like being a pop star. The position and the glamour and money associated with it does strange things to people. At Kensington Palace, a number of women, including female staff, were thought to have flirted with William. One or two female members of staff were moved to other duties as a result.

William's rather awkward, even inhibited personality – an inheritance from his father – was baffling for the more open, spontaneous Meghan Markle. A member of staff recalled Meghan asking, 'Why do William and Charles sound so serious all the time?' 'She used to make jokes about Harry not having the same parents as William, as, she insisted, "Harry isn't pompous at all. He's chill."'

Kate inevitably sees a different side of William and she enjoys ribbing him about his family. She insists that, as he gets older, William increasingly looks like his great-great-great-grandfather Edward VII and she likes teasing him about the fact that his stepmother Camilla is descended from Edward VII's favourite mistress.

According to one of William's advisers, the prince is more than capable of getting his own back. He says:

Before Kate realised that as a senior royal you have to dress carefully, having taken advice, she once bought an outfit that William considered inappropriate. He told Kate she looked as if in order to dress she'd just run through a charity shop covered in superglue. Everyone thought this was very funny, including, to her credit, Kate.

But like King Charles and Prince Harry, William has his needier side. A former Kensington Palace maid says: 'Kate had to explain many of the things that parents outside the royal family do with their children as a matter of course.'

* * *

Various members of the couple's former staff agree that, while she was a working royal, Meghan was focused on how she could become the best-known and most-loved member of the royal family. 'She really did have a messiah complex,' said one.

> I don't mean that in a critical way because all her big ideas were about doing good. She once said, 'What Diana started I want to finish,' and we took that to mean she wanted to become a sort of globetrotting champion of the poor and the marginalised. She has managed to do this to some extent, but she really wanted to do it as a princess and with the full backing of the royal family but on a part-time basis.

According to one of Elizabeth II's former courtiers,

> Buckingham Palace became really worried when they became aware that Meghan had plans for her life as a working royal that were not going to be part of a general strategy agreed with the staff – she just wanted to do her own thing, which is fair enough if you're not a member of a tightly controlled institution, but it was never going to be acceptable that Meghan should outshine Princess Anne, Prince Charles [as he then was] and Elizabeth

the Queen. Quite rightly, Elizabeth always had to be the centre and focus of everything the royal family did and I don't think Meghan understood why that had to make her do things she didn't want to do. She didn't understand that when you join the royal family, you don't do as you please, you do as you're told. In a sense, you become a servant of the family.

Any new arrival in the royal family finds a curious mix. There are staff to carry out most private, day-to-day menial tasks, but the public-facing work of the royals is decided by the courtiers and senior staff and senior royals. Meghan undoubtedly felt constrained by this and she felt that both she and Harry needed to break out – to still be royals and still be working royals but do their own thing without consulting the big royal machine. But this was never going to be acceptable.

Harry was delighted by the possibility of freedom, of doing things differently, that Meghan introduced into his life. Senior staff begged him to intervene with Meghan to try to make her toe the line, but by all accounts this was the beginning of what staffers describe as 'Harry's tendency to defend anything and everything Meghan says or does'.

A bigger problem for Meghan when she was a core member of the royal family was that she both loved having everything done for her by the domestic staff and also hated it. This is why when she returned to the United States, she employed only a small number of staff and asked her mother to take charge of the childcare for Archie and Lilibet.

A former Kensington Palace staffer says:

Through absolutely no fault of her own, Meghan wasn't always great with her staff – she just wasn't used to it as Harry was. So, one minute she would be really friendly, perhaps over-friendly, with the staff, hugging everyone and trying to make friends with them, and the next she would be irritated by the fact that they wouldn't respond instantly at all times of the day and night. At times it got so bad that I heard one of the senior staff mumble that Meghan should really have been employed in the palace kitchens, so there was some snobbery.

It's true that her nickname for a while was the Duchess of Difficult, but she had other, friendlier nicknames, including Mystic Meg, which came about because she was so New Agey, so woke, about so many things. She could be difficult, because she was finding life difficult – trying to feel her way and work out the intricacies of a positively medieval labyrinthine system. It's not even easy for people who come from backgrounds far closer to the royal family, such as Princess Diana. Even she was shocked by the complexities and jealousy within the royal family. For Meghan, it was almost incomprehensible because she couldn't understand why Charles, for example, was so formal with his mother. She once said, 'But they're mother and son – why are they so completely stiff with each other?' She spotted the fact that, as is so often the case, members of the British royal family are actually usually more comfortable with their staff, their servants, than they are with each other!

A lot of it is tied up with the fact that their lives are not their own. Meghan quite rightly hated the fact that when she was in Nottingham Cottage, she had to agree well in advance what time she might leave for an appointment or an event and she had to make sure she didn't leave at the same time as, or clash in any way with, a more senior royal leaving the palace.

So how did Catherine Middleton negotiate these difficult matters with staff and family relationships? She too had no real experience of the intricate royal machine and very little experience of having servants. The answer was summed up neatly by a former member of the Kensington Palace staff:

Kate is someone who slowly and carefully absorbs the atmosphere of a place, the relationship between people and the rules. She doesn't jump in straight away and try to change everything to suit her way of thinking. She bides her time and is very intelligent and intuitive about other people, what they do and how they behave. She was also coached – not just by William, who wanted Kate to avoid the problems his mother had encountered, but also by the staff.

Kate was always happy to accept advice both from the lower staff, with whom she got on very well, and from the more senior courtiers – and she took advice from the courtiers even though some of them were initially very snooty about her.

Just as Princess Margaret's husband was sneered at for being a nobody, so Kate had to put up with something similar. In many ways it was just the same as the kind of backbiting gossipy criticism that Meghan had to put up with, but Kate is actually a much stronger person than Meghan in many ways. Some people thought it wasn't strength but a sort of passivity – that was one of the bugbears between Meghan and Kate. Meghan wanted Kate to be feistier and make her own mark. But what Meghan saw as Kate being pushed around, Kate saw as an essential part of being a member of the royal family.

Kate's view of Meghan was always implied rather than spoken, I think. It was that Meghan thought she knew better than an institution that had been in business for a thousand years and more. Kate was never going to buy that.

A member of the Kensington Palace communications team added, 'Meghan thought Kate was just too eager to please, too much a goody-two-shoes girl.'

But for all these criticisms and implied criticisms, it remains true that Meghan had her supporters at Kensington Palace. Many of the ordinary staff liked the fact that she was feisty and wanted to change things for the better. Others felt that making changes was not an acceptable role for a complete outsider.

They [the older, public school-educated advisers] really had it in for Meghan and to be fair to her she really stood up to them, but of course if you make waves in the royal family, the senior royals will always back the courtiers, because in many cases the senior royals have been friends with the courtiers since childhood.

Here, as so often in royal history, we see the royal family and the aristocracy closing ranks against the disruptive intruder who does not share their ancient connections and does not share their basic assumptions. A former member of the Kensington Palace staff said:

When someone arrives from the United States and tries to change things, the old guard really don't like it. And the old guard are terrific snobs – they have to be less obviously snobbish today, but it's still there.

I can tell you that if William had wanted to marry Meghan Markle, it would've been a step too far both for the royal family and for all the courtiers and advisers. It was OK for Harry to marry Meghan, because Harry was never going to be king. The courtiers and ladies in waiting and communications teams thought Meghan would keep Harry out of trouble; give him something to focus on. In fact, in many ways, they'd have been happy for him to marry *anyone* just to see him settled and to keep him out of trouble. They thought he'd just go away and have children and live at Windsor or wherever and be happy.

One particular courtier I won't name actually said this to me – he said Harry was always a problem. After his military service, what on earth was he going to do? The courtiers and other senior advisers knew that Harry didn't really want to do the usual royal round, partly because he got so fed up with all the handshaking and the small talk, but also because he felt continually that he was second best.

The strongly held view among current and former royal staff is that when Meghan arrived on the scene, she quickly convinced Harry that he was being neglected, sidelined and undervalued. She felt she was just standing up for her husband, telling 'her truth' and encouraging him to tell his, but this was seen as deeply disruptive in a royal family that relies not just on the staff doing what they're told but on the royals themselves doing what history tells them they should do.

Meghan was a moderniser by nature. Someone who wanted to get things done and change the status quo. She was actually very good at persuading some of the staff, even the junior staff, to be very much on her side and that too caused problems. According to my sources, Meghan became especially friendly and close to one particular member of staff, who was really quite junior, and even this was seen as inappropriate by the senior royals.

With Kensington Palace staff split into for Meghan and against Meghan, the atmosphere was one of swirling rumour, gossip and backbiting – an atmosphere in which the truth became blurred and point of view became objective fact.

The famous row over the bridesmaid's dress and whether Kate made Meghan cry or vice versa is a case in point, as a former member of staff recalls:

> You remember all the fuss about Meghan being accused of making Kate cry when they had a dispute about Charlotte's bridesmaid's dress? Well, I can tell you that all the papers and commentators got this wrong – the truth is that as with many of these spats between sisters, brothers or even sisters-in-law, *both*

sides were really upset. I'm amazed everyone didn't see that this was the most likely explanation. If you think about it, weddings are one of the most stressful things you can go through apart from bereavement, and royal weddings are up there in the stress stratosphere. The truth is that during the discussions about the bridesmaid's dress Meghan said a few things she regretted and Kate said a few things she later regretted but it was all in the heat of the moment. Both women were crying their eyes out! Whenever this sort of thing happens in the royal family, traditionally no one says anything publicly about it so it rarely reaches the media, but on this occasion all sorts of other grievances meant that what was really nothing but a storm in a teacup reached the media and became a big issue. The other thing people forget is that when a private royal argument or row reaches the media, it gets subtly altered and usually made more significant than it really is. But even the royals tend to believe what they read in the newspapers if it suits them, so the incident with the bridesmaid's dress became a kind of marker for all the other problems that Meghan had with Kate and with William and other members of the family.

Meghan had a very typically American view of the royal family before she joined – for her, the royal family was about castles, glittering balls and limitless wealth and ease. Harry seems to have spent little time explaining exactly how strange and demanding his family really are – but then perhaps that is no surprise given that Harry has never really been able to step outside and look at himself and his family with an objective eye.

Having everything done for you throughout your life by staff gives you a complacent air, something several of Harry's former Kensington Palace advisers have noted. Before Meghan, Harry was annoyed by press attention but not unduly; indeed, he often revelled in his fame and his ability to attract girlfriends.

He also failed ever to question his own position as one of the elite, so he was deeply shocked at Meghan's reaction when she discovered, for example, that he was not personally hugely wealthy. As one member of staff put it, 'She expected a billionaire and she got a millionaire.'

It was perfectly understandable that, coming from an American background, Meghan might imagine that Prince Harry, the brother of a future king, should have billions. So, when she discovered that Harry was only worth around £20 million, she needed to reassess many other assumptions she'd made about this strange new family. Then came Nottingham Cottage.

Meghan had simply assumed that after her marriage she would live either in Buckingham Palace or at Windsor Castle. It was a deep shock to find herself in this small house with no live-in staff in the grounds of Kensington Palace. Harry would never have objected to this – a small but rather beautiful house in the grounds of a famous palace hardly seemed to Harry the equivalent to being forced to live in a shed at the end of the garden. But for Meghan things were more complex. She saw Kate and William living in a vast apartment (actually a substantial house) just a few yards away in Kensington Palace itself and with teams of servants on hand day and night.

As one member of staff who helped out regularly at Nottingham Cottage recalled:

Starting life as a member of the royal family in Nottingham Cottage was the beginning of all Meghan's troubles – she felt it was so small that it must be a reflection on how the royal family were belittling her husband. She just didn't understand that real royals don't care much about houses and material possessions because having always had them they take them for granted.

This early upset was compounded by a vague feeling that the Kensington Palace staff tended to treat Harry as less important than his brother. A member of the comms team who was particularly close to Meghan said:

Meghan spotted immediately that Harry wasn't quite as central to things as his brother William. This was the start of the whole grievance thing about being the spare. I don't think Harry had even thought much about the fact that he was a spare until well into his marriage. Meghan managed to give him more perspective because she could see the family from the outside and her experience of growing up was so totally different and, with her mixed-race heritage, as we now have to describe it, she was acutely sensitive to how people behaved towards each other; in fact, I think she was over-sensitive on Harry's behalf and convinced herself he was being treated as completely unimportant.

With this in mind, it is easy to see that Harry soon saw in Meghan someone who would be his champion, when, arguably, he didn't need one. A retired member of the Kensington Palace staff remembers:

Before Meghan came along, Harry had his down days, certainly, but no worse than anyone else in his strange, privileged yet restricted world. He was normally a very polite, reasonably happy young man. He'd got past the stage of getting drunk in nightclubs and was focusing far more on his few reliable friends from school and from the military and he seemed quite happy with life. He got on exceptionally well with his sister-in-law Kate and with his brother. It was only when he began to feel that he was being treated as a second-class citizen that the anger began to build up and then the rows – and there were a lot of rows – and the eventual split.

According to numerous palace sources, William couldn't understand why Harry had changed so much. When they were growing up, they both enjoyed polo, pheasant shooting and other country sports and there was no sense when Harry turned up at any of these events that he was treated differently from his brother. One source says, 'When you have teams of servants looking after you and you're driven wherever you want to go at whatever time you want to go and you have no money worries, it never occurs to you that you're not a very special person. And that was Harry's position before his marriage.'

Servant gossip at the time Harry began to fall out with his family was really based around the question: why can't he just be happy with his luxurious playboy life? One of the senior courtiers tried to explain to Harry that he was actually much better off than his brother, because William would never be able to escape the full focus of the media, especially when he became king. Harry, by contrast, could live a life where some of the time he had all the benefits of being a private citizen and the rest of the time he had all the benefits of being a senior member of the royal family. But increasingly Harry couldn't see this.

One of Harry's senior aides, now retired, says:

Harry went from being pretty easy-going to being not exactly difficult but more disgruntled. We had meetings about events he was planning to attend and I increasingly got the feeling his mind was elsewhere – fair enough, after Meghan's arrival, he was concerned about her welfare, but it was as if his job now was not to attend events, which is what the senior royals always do as their core activity, and instead he saw his core activity as being with Meghan and increasingly adopting her views of the world. Some people would say he was just being a loyal husband, but the team, the staff, found the whole thing baffling.

It's perhaps too easy to paint Harry as the sort of rootless character who was always looking for the kind of self-assurance Meghan Markle undoubtedly possesses, but that is how it seemed to the comms team and other staff at Kensington Palace. Yet there is another side to the story, as one former staffer relates:

Harry was one of the easiest and nicest people to work for – I think you would find all the domestic and communications staff would agree on that, and they felt rather sad as he began to move away from being a key member of the royal family. That terrible modern word 'woke' has often been used and although I don't like it, I can see why it is applied to Harry – he did become far more concerned about social issues and the rights of minorities than he'd ever been before Meghan's arrival. Some of the youngest staff at Kensington Palace would've applauded this, no doubt, but the older staff thought he'd become a tree-hugging lefty! They saw it as Harry rejecting the values and traditions of his family. And the really senior staff thought, oh my God, here we go again – Meghan is Mrs Simpson come back to haunt us!

Another former member of Meghan's staff recalls the awkwardness and hilarity of early meetings with the new princess:

Well, when Meghan had meetings at Kensington Palace, it was extraordinary because she was so confident that you could see she wanted to run the meeting rather than learn about the royal family through the meeting. I think this was typical of what happened throughout her time at Kensington Palace and then Windsor. She was a great believer in grabbing the bull by the horns – except the royal family is not really a bull!

Meghan tended to get on well with the junior staff and the domestic staff, who were never a threat and to a large extent did whatever she asked them to do.

All agree that, newly arrived at Kensington Palace, Meghan must have felt very much as Captain Peter Townsend or Antony

Armstrong-Jones felt in an earlier age – like them, she was slightly looked down on by the very grand courtiers who were and still are the closest officials to the senior royals. Some people can cope with this – Kate Middleton is perhaps the supreme example – but others try to fight back, which is what Meghan clearly did.

'You've got to hand it to her,' says a former member of her staff, 'she really is a fighter.'

One member of staff who worked often at Nottingham Cottage says:

> Meghan seemed frequently to be slightly dissatisfied – she really didn't like Nottingham Cottage, even though most of us would've given anything to live there. And she absolutely insisted on being involved with every detail [of her royal life]. I thought she was quite demanding – she probably thought she was being perfectly reasonable, but asking for things very late in the day or very early in the morning isn't the sort of thing that you do when people are already working long hours to please you.

Elizabeth II famously hated disturbing her staff out of hours. But after so many decades as Queen, she knew exactly how to treat everyone to get the best out of them. For Meghan, starting out negotiating these things was far more difficult.

The irony, given all that has been written about Harry being the 'spare', is that at Kensington Palace, it was clearly Meghan who felt she could not find her place; she too was a spare. But then the royal family has always been about precedence, and precedence is based on the accident of birth. Hard work and determination cut no ice in the royal family – as Meghan learned to her cost.

Conclusion

Hail and farewell

'At one time, Prince Harry employed two full-time
staff just to deal with his fan mail.'
– PALACE OFFICIAL, AUTHOR INTERVIEW

In the great arguments about allowing women to work and giving women the vote, arguments that reached fever pitch with the suffragette movement, the justification usually given for maintaining the status quo was that women were delicate, spiritual creatures whose pure minds focused on higher things and whose refined natures should not be sullied by the sordid cares of work and politics.

Queen Victoria was one of the most violent defenders of the old order. Writing to Prime Minister William Gladstone in 1870, she said, 'The Queen is most anxious to enlist everyone in checking this wicked folly of "Women's Rights". It is a subject that makes the Queen so furious that she cannot contain herself.'

When Victoria, Gladstone and Parliament discussed women's rights, but especially the right to work and to vote, they were thinking solely about middle-class and aristocratic women. Working-class women had always worked – but so far as politicians and the royal family were concerned, the working-class woman barely existed and where she did exist, she did so only insofar as she was prepared to work for those delicate, spiritual women who struggled to get off the sofa each day.

What lay behind this attitude was an unthinking assumption that working-class women, who made up the vast bulk of royal domestic servants, had no interior mental life at all. The royal family, like the aristocracy, thought of those who worked in their kitchens and gardens as 'simple machines or simpletons', as one former maid interviewed by the present author put it. 'It was almost as if we existed as a carthorse would exist, or a piece of furniture.'

This perhaps explains why Queen Mary was so baffled and hurt when Marion Crawford, nanny to Princesses Elizabeth and Margaret, asked for time off to get married. Queen Mary said, 'But the children can't possibly manage without you.'

At the other end of the scale, the honours for which courtiers and other royal servants once clamoured have become to some extent meaningless baubles awarded by the royal family to each other and to their friends and relations.

What might have been taken seriously in the past is now seen as pointless gesturing. When Queen Victoria appointed her husband Ranger of Windsor Great Park (at a salary of £500 per annum), the newspapers reported what was seen then as a signal and well-deserved honour. How much time Prince Albert actually spent patrolling Windsor Great Park is difficult now to calculate, but such an appointment might be greeted in the twenty-first century with scepticism if not derision.

Monarchs can no longer take the approbation of the public for granted. The result is that numerous honours in the gift of the royal family are now simply given to other members of the royal family, just as Victoria gave her husband that lucrative job as Warden of Windsor Great Park.

Handing baubles round has become almost absurd. In 2024, King Charles made Catherine Middleton (already Princess of Wales) a Royal Companion of the Order of the Companions of Honour. According to the royal family's own website, this is a special award granted to 'those who have made a major contribution to the arts, science, medicine, or government lasting over a long period of time'. Fearing, no doubt, that she might feel left out, Charles made his wife, Queen Camilla, Grand Master of the Order of the British Empire. He also decided to make the Duchess of Gloucester a Royal Lady Companion of the Most Noble Order of the Garter. Charles himself is dripping in titles: he is an air chief marshal, a field marshal and an admiral, to name but three.

The proliferation of awards, honours and titles parallels the proliferation of royal servant jobs. We have seen how having one and a half men per job was the rule in the past, but even today the royal family is always under pressure – largely the pressure of tradition – to employ too many staff. The nursery is a case in point.

When Catherine Middleton married Prince William, she vowed to cut out many if not all of the jobs traditionally associated with the nursery, so that her children would not have the kind of royal upbringing where infant princes and princesses bond most closely with their paid caregivers and grow up, as William and Harry grew up after the death of their mother, feeling little emotional connection to their actual parents.

Catherine was determined as far as possible to look after her children herself, but even Catherine's determination to do things differently could not outweigh the pressure of tradition – and that pressure was brought to bear by the aristocratic courtiers and indeed by the senior royals themselves. This was combined with sheer exhaustion, and what started as an admirable attempt to look after her young children herself ended to a large extent when both William and Kate realised that pressure from above and from their work schedule meant a more traditional approach had to be adopted. A former staffer put it bluntly: 'They were appalled at how tired they were.'

That said, we should remember that Kate may not have won the war but she certainly won many of the battles. Despite the disapproval of many of the palace old guard, she has spent what many royal insiders see as a shocking amount of time doing the normal childcare tasks that in the past were farmed out to paid staff. But even Kate acknowledges that if you join the royal family, you have to obey some if not most of the rules. A nanny and a nursery maid for the children were unavoidable, but Kate was very careful to choose a nanny she felt she could work closely with. The result was the appointment in 2014 of Maria Teresa Turrion Borrallo.

Borrallo studied at the prestigious Norland College, which

insists on a curiously old-fashioned brown uniform that includes a bowler hat. Norland nannies with ten years' experience are paid around £100,000 per annum (in 2023) and they are inevitably the nanny of choice for the world's super-rich, whether Chinese billionaires, Russian oligarchs or members of the royal family.

In true Mary Poppins style, Norland nannies are even taught martial arts – including how to use a pram as a weapon to evade kidnappers – and they are taught how to drive safely at high speed.

Old ideas about social class formed part of the original inspiration for Norland College founder Emily Ward: she explained that the uniforms were designed to make sure that a Norland nanny could never be mistaken for a housemaid.

Given that George, Charlotte and Louis are surrounded by staff anyway, one might ask why they even need a nanny? The question becomes more acute when one remembers how, even before her cancer diagnosis, Kate was increasingly focused on her children and she and William were involved in far fewer engagements than other senior royals such as Princess Anne.

If we think it is bizarre to have a family in our midst whose servant-bolstered lives are essentially drawn straight from the eighteenth century, it is perhaps even stranger that the family itself buys into the fantasy, a fantasy that relies on being seen to have most practical daily tasks carried out by hundreds of servants.

The truth is that royal servants are the lights on the royal Christmas tree, and the royal Christmas tree must be bigger and brighter than any other tree. It's the vast edifice of the royal family – the houses and palaces, the estates and the countless servants – that helps ensure the royal family can be seen, as the late Queen Elizabeth II once put it, to be believed.

Servants at their best – or at their most foolish, depending on your viewpoint – give their whole lives to their duties. According to one of her footmen, the late Queen once said, 'We work for the country throughout our lives and many of those who work for us do exactly the same.'

Royal service is a culture of mutual dependence, where some servants become so dazzled by their royal masters that they can never leave. In an interview with the present author, a journalist and former member of Prince Andrew's staff said, 'The key thing about Andrew's private secretary from 2012, Amanda Thirsk, was that she was so loyal to him it was sometimes impossible to see where she ended and Andrew began!'

Staff begin to identify with their masters, and the masters find they cannot do without their staff.

King Charles, for example, insists on muffins and eggs every afternoon at teatime. He has never once cooked his own eggs and muffins. Because, like many people, Charles is fussy about how his eggs are cooked, and because eggs are notoriously difficult to get just right, he insists that six eggs should be cooked so that at least two will be just as he likes them.

Henry VIII and Queen Victoria would see this as perfectly reasonable behaviour, and for senior royals in the twenty-first century it is still perfectly reasonable behaviour.

Despite the modern royals living very much as their ancestors lived in this respect, we have nonetheless come a long way. When she was eight years old, for example, one of Princess Anne's favourite pastimes was to walk back and forth in front of one of the guards at Buckingham Palace, knowing that each time she did so, the guard would have to present arms. No royal child would get away with this today.

But in terms of servant relationships, revolution was definitely in the air when Meghan Markle married Prince Harry. One key element of Meghan's time at Kensington Palace that caused consternation among the old guard – the traditional aristocratic courtiers – was, as we have seen, Meghan's delightful habit of hugging everyone with whom she came into regular contact.

Meghan may have been demanding in some ways, but her deep democratic instincts also made her affectionate to all those members of her staff she liked. For the other senior royals, however, this was a step too far – over-familiarity with the staff was worse than rudeness to them. And the hugging didn't stop with the servants. Kate, William and Charles tended to flinch when she moved in for a hug. Meghan was understandably hurt, as everyone apparently hugs everyone in California.

If it was unseemly to hug servants and other royals, Meghan went even further when she tried and sometimes succeeded in hugging senior courtiers.

One member of Meghan's team recalled in an interview with the present author that

Meghan has had a very bad press, but when I worked for her, she was absolutely charming – very informal, courteous and warm. And she did something no other royal had ever done – she gave me a hug. But I was careful always to be deferential to her and if she asked for something to be done, I did it. People who tried to persuade her to do things she didn't want to do had a much harder time of it. But she really disliked the hierarchy, the rules, many of which do seem pretty pointless and exist really only so that the relative status of each senior royal is protected. And the senior royals are such a sensitive bunch – if one gets a gold pen or a new car, they all want one. Meghan thought they behaved like babies!

The royals' line in the twenty-first century is that they are moving with the times. They have slimmed down and will have fewer working royals – and, as a result, fewer servants, whether they be courtiers, public relations professionals or maids and footmen.

But this is just the public face of the royal servant world. Some servants carry out work that would shock many of us, but they are essential to at least one extraordinary feudal practice.

If you die in most places in England and Wales and you have left no will and have no known next of kin, your assets go to the Treasury – in other words, to the government, to be spent much as general taxes are spent. But if you die inside the medieval boundaries of the Lancashire County Palatine, your money will go to the Duchy of Lancaster, the property empire owned by the King.

As a *Guardian* newspaper report explained:

In the Duchy of Cornwall, the Prince of Wales [Prince William] benefits from a similar arrangement. Both duchies claim the net proceeds go to charity, but research ... has found that a hefty chunk of the £60 million collected by the Duchy of Lancaster between 2010–2020 has been used ... to refurbish properties the duchy lets out commercially. Unclaimed estates of former miners from the Lake District are being used to spruce up the royal property portfolio.

The system operates under a medieval rule known as *bona vacantia*.

The servants who administer the duchy, like all royal servants, from courtiers to kitchen maids, obey one rule and one rule only: maximise the pleasures and profits of the royal family. And in that respect, not much has changed in more than a thousand years.

Bibliography

Alexandra, Queen of Yugoslavia, *Prince Philip: A Family Portrait*, Hodder and Stoughton, 1960

Alice, Princess, Duchess of Gloucester, *Memories of Ninety Years*, Collins & Brown, 1991

Alice, Princess, *For My Grandchildren*, Evans Brothers, 1966

Andersson, Peter K., *Fool*, Princeton University Press, 2023

Anonymous, *The Private Life of the Queen by One of Her Servants*, C. Arthur Pearson, 1898

Appleyard, John, *William of Orange and the English Revolution*, Dent, 1908

Armin, Robert, *Collected Works*, Johnson Reprint Company, 1972

Aronson, Theo, *Prince Eddy and the Homosexual Underworld*, Lume Publishing, 2020

Ascham, Roger, *The Schoolmaster*, Cassell, 1909Ashdown, Dulcie M., *Royal Children*, Hale, 1979

Asquith, Lady Cynthia, *Haply I may remember*, James Barrie, 1950

Asquith, Lady Cynthia, *The King's Daughters*, Hutchinson, 1937

Aston, Sir George, *The Duke of Connaught and Strathearn: A Life*, Harrap, 1929

Bagehot, Walter, *The British Constitution*, ed. Paul Smith, Cambridge University Press, 2001Bain, Joseph (ed.), *Calendar of Letters and Papers Relating to the Affairs of the Borders of England and Scotland*, 2 vols, Edinburgh, 1894–95

Baker, Richard, *A Chronicle of the Kings of England*, London, 1653

Balderson, Eileen, *Backstairs Life in a Country House*, David & Charles, 1982

Baldry, A. L., *Royal Palaces*, The Studio, 1935

Basford, Elisabeth, *Princess Mary*, History Press, 2021

Bathurst, Benjamin (ed.), *Mary II and Anne: Letters of Two Queens*, Holden & Co., 1925

Battiscombe, Georgina, *Queen Alexandra*, Constable, 1969

Baxter, Stephen B., *William III*, Longmans, 1966

Baxter, Stephen B., *William III and the Defence of European Liberty 1650–1702*, Harcourt, 1966

Bayne-Powell, Rosamond, *The English Child in the Eighteenth Century*, John Murray, 1939

BB (pseud.) and Denys Watkins-Pitchford (illus.), *A Child Alone*, Michael Joseph, 1978

Beamish, Noel, *A Royal Scandal*, Hale, 1966

Beaton, Cecil, *The Royal Portraits*, ed. Roy Strong, Thames & Hudson, 1988

Bennett, Daphne, *Queen Victoria's Children*, Gollancz, 1980

Bennett, Daphne, *Vicky: Princess Royal of England and German Empress*, Collins, 1971

Benson, A. C., and Viscount Esher (eds), *The Letters of Queen Victoria: A Selection from Her Majesty's Correspondence*, John Murray, 1907

Berg, Maxine, *Luxury and Pleasure in Eighteenth-Century England*, Oxford University Press, 2005

Bergeron, David, *King James and Letters of Homoerotic Desire*, University of Iowa Press, 1999

Bloch, Michael, *The Duchess of Windsor*, Weidenfeld & Nicolson, 1996

Bolitho, Hector (ed.), *The Prince Consort and his Brother: 100 New Letters*, Cobden-Sanderson, 1933

Boorde, Andrew, *The Fyrst Boke of the Introduction of Knowledge*, ed. F. J. Furnivall, Early English Text Society, 1870

Bower, Tom, *Revenge: Meghan, Harry and the War Between the Windsors*, Blink, 2022

Boyd, William K. (ed.), *Calendar of the State Papers Relating to Scotland and Mary, Queen of Scots, 1547–1603*, Edinburgh, 1898–1969

Broadley, Alexander Meyrick, *The Boyhood of a Great King, 1841–58: An Account of the Early Years of the Life of His Majesty Edward VII*, Harper, 1906

Brown, Craig, *Ma'am Darling: 99 Glimpses of Princess Margaret*, Fourth Estate, 2017

Brown, Craig and Cunliffe, L., *The Book of Royal Trivia*, Routledge, 1982

Brown, Tina, *The Palace Papers*, Century, 2022

Bruce, Marie-Louise, *The Youth of Henry VIII*, Collins, 1978

Bryant, Arthur, *Charles II*, Longmans Green, 1931

Bryant, Chris, *Entitled: A Critical History of the British Aristocracy*, Doubleday, 2007

Burn, Richard, *The Justice of the Peace and Parish Officer*, A. Millar, 1755

Burnet, Bishop Gilbert, *History of His Own Time*, William Smith, 1838

Burnet, Bishop Gilbert, *History of His Own Time*, Clarendon, 1823

Burrell, Paul, *The Way We Were: Remembering Diana*, HarperCollins, 2006

Campbell, James et al., *The Anglo Saxons*, Penguin, 1991

Campbell, Judith Anne, *Portrait of a Princess*, Cassell, 1970

Carey, M. C., *Princess Mary*, Nisbet & Co., 1922

Carter, Miranda, *Anthony Blunt: His Lives*, Pan, 2002

Castiglione, Baldassare, *The Book of the Courtier*, trs. Thomas Hoby, Dent, 1970

Chance, Michael, *Our Princesses and their Dogs*, John Murray, 1936

Chandler, Glenn, *The Sins of Jack Saul*, Grosvenor House, 2016
Channon, Sir Henry 'Chips', *Diaries*, Weidenfeld & Nicolson, 1993

Chapman, Hester W., *Mary II*, Jonathan Cape, 1953

Chapman, Hester W., *The Tragedy of Charles II*, Jonathan Cape, 1964

Chenevix Trench, Charles, *George II*, Allen Lane, 1973

Claydon, A. M., T. Claydon and M. A. Speck, *William and Mary*, Oxford University Press, 2007

Clayton, Michael, *Prince Charles: Horseman*, Stanley Paul, 1987

Cook, Andrew, *Prince Eddy: The King Britain Never Had*, History Press, 2011

Courtney, Nicholas, *Royal Children*, Dent, 1982

Crawford, Marion, *The Little Princesses*, Cassell, 1950

Curzon, Catherine, *Life in the Georgian Court*, Pen & Sword, 2016

Daiken, Leslie, *Children's Games Throughout the Year*, Batsford, 1949

Dalton, John Neale (ed.), *Cruise of HMS Bacchante 1879–82*, 2 vols, Macmillan, 1886

Darton, F. J. Harvey, *Children's Books in England: Five Centuries of Social Life*, rev. Brian Alderson, Cambridge University Press, 2005

Davies, Philip (ed.), *Lost London, 1870–1945*, Transatlantic Press, 2009

Dempster, Nigel, *HRH The Princess Margaret: A Life Unfulfilled*, Chivers, 1982

Dempster, Nigel and Peter Evans, *Behind Palace Doors*, Orion, 1993

Dennison, Matthew, *Queen Victoria: A Life of Contradictions*, William Collins, 2013

Dobson, Austin, *Old Kensington Palace and Other Papers*, Humphrey Milford, 1926

Donaldson, Frances, *Edward VIII*, Weidenfeld & Nicolson, 1974

Drummond, J. C., and Anne Wilbraham, *The Englishman's Food: Five Centuries of English Diet*, Pimlico, 1999

Duff, David, *The Shy Princess*, Evans Brothers, 1958

Dunlop, O. Jocelyn, *English Apprenticeship and Child Labour*, Fisher Unwin, 1975

Edgar, Donald, *Prince Andrew*, A. Barker, 1980

Epton, Nina, *Queen Victoria and her Daughters*, Weidenfeld & Nicolson, 1971

Faulkner, Thomas, *History and Antiquities of Kensington*, T. Egerton, 1820

Field, Ophelia, *The Favourite: Sarah, Duchess of Marlborough*, Hodder, 2002

Finch, Barbara Clay, *Lives of the Princesses of Wales*, Remington & Co., 1883

Fisher, Graham, *Prince Andrew*, W. H. Allen, 1981

Fisher, Graham and Heather, *Monarchy and the Royal Family*, Hale, 1979

Flanders, Judith, *Consuming Passions: Leisure and Pleasure in Victorian Britain*, Harper, 2006

Foot, P. W. R., *The Child in the Twentieth Century*, Cassell, 1968

Fox, James, *Five Sisters: The Langhornes of Virginia*, Simon & Schuster, 2000

Frankland, Noble, *Prince Henry: Duke of Gloucester*, Weidenfeld & Nicolson, 1980

French, Russell, *The Ancestry of Her Majesty Queen Victoria and His Royal Highness Prince Albert*, William Pickering, 1841

Fryman, Olivia (ed.), *Kensington Palace: Art, Architecture and Society*, Yale University Press, 2018

Fulford, Roger (ed.), *Dearest Child: Letters between Queen Victoria and the Princess Royal 1858–61*, Evans Brothers, 1958

Fulford, Roger (ed.), *Dearest Mama: Letters between Queen Victoria and the Crown Princess of Prussia 1861–64*, Evans Brothers, 1968

Fulford, Roger, *The Prince Consort*, Macmillan, 1949

Fulford, Roger, *Royal Dukes*, Duckworth, 1933

Fulford, Roger, *The Wicked Uncles*, Pan, 1968

Furnivall, F. J. (ed.), *Manners and Meals in Olden Time*, Early English Text Society, 1868

Gathorne-Hardy, Jonathan, *The Rise and Fall of the British Nanny*, Hodder and Stoughton, 1972

Glasheen, Joan, *Secret People of the Palaces*, Batsford, 1998

Glenconner, *Anne, Lady in Waiting*, Hodder, 2020

Godfrey, Elizabeth, *English Children in the Olden Time*, Methuen, 1907

Gore, John, *King George V: A Personal Memoir*, John Murray, 1941

Gough, Richard, *The History of Myddle*, Caliban Books, 1979

Graham, Eleanor, *The Making of a Queen: Victoria at Kensington Palace*, Cape, 1940

Gray, Annie, *The Greedy Queen*, Profile Books, 2017

Greig, Hannah, *The Beau Monde*, Oxford University Press, 2013

Hadlow, Janice, *The Strangest Family: The Private Lives of George III, Queen Charlotte and the Hanoverians*, William Collins, 2014

Haley, K. H. D., *William of Orange and the English Opposition*, Clarendon, 1953

Hamilton, Anthony, *Memoirs of the Count de Grammont*, Bodley Head, 1928

Hardman, Robert, *Charles III*, Macmillan, 2024

Hardman, Robert, *Queen of Our Times: The Life of Elizabeth II*, Pan, 2023

Hartmann, Cyril Hughes, *The King My Brother: Henrietta Anne and Charles II*, Heinemann, 1954

Hatton, Ragnhild, *George I*, Yale University Press, 1978

Hecht, J. Jean, *The Domestic Servant Class in Eighteenth-Century England*, Routledge, 1956

Hentzner, Paul and Sir R. Naunton, *Travels in England during the reign of Queen Elizabeth*, Cassell, 1889

Hervey, John, *Memoirs*, ed. Romney Sedgwick, Penguin, 1984

Hervey, Lady Mary Lepel, *Letters*, ed. John Wilson, Bibliobazaar, 2009

Hibbert, Christopher, *Charles I*, Weidenfeld & Nicolson, 1968

Hibbert, Christopher, *Edward VII: The Last Victorian King*, Griffin, 2007

Hoare, Philip, *England's Lost Eden: Adventures in a Victorian Utopia*, Harper, 2010

Hoey, Brian, *Anne, The Princess Royal*, Grafton, 1989

Holden, Anthony, *Charles, Prince of Wales*, Pan, 1980

Hole, Christina, *English Home Life 1500 to 1800*, Batsford, 1947

Honeycombe, Gordon, *Royal Wedding*, Michael Joseph, 1981

Horn, Pamela, *Life Below Stairs in the Twentieth Century*, Amberley, 2014

Horne, Eric, *More Winks*, T. W. Lawrie, 1932

Hoskings, W. G., *The Making of the English Landscape*, Penguin, 1970

Huggett, Frank E., *Life Below Stairs*, John Murray, 1977

Hunt, Leigh, *Essays*, Forgotten Books, 2018

Hunt, Leigh, *Old Court Suburb, or, Memorials of Kensington*, John Murray, 1860

Hunt, Margaret, 'Women in Eighteenth-Century Europe', *European History Quarterly*, Vol. 45, No. 1

Hyde, H. Montgomery, *The Cleveland Street Scandal*, W. H. Allen, 1976

Impey, Edward, *Kensington Palace: The Official Illustrated History*, Merrell, 2003

Jackman, Nancy, *The Cook's Tale*, Sceptre, 2012

Jesse, John Heneage, *Memoirs of the English Court*, Bohn, 1857

Johnson, Dr Samuel, *Journal of a Tour to the Hebrides*, Constable, 1898

Jordan, Don and Michael Walsh, *The King's Bed: Ambition and Intimacy in the Court of Charles II*, Pegasus, 2017

Judd, Denis, *Prince Philip: A Biography*, Michael Joseph, 1980

Junor, Penny, *Charles*, Sidgwick & Jackson, 1987

Keay, Douglas, *Elizabeth I*, Century, 1991

Kennedy Jr, David, *Children*, Batsford, 1971

Kelly, Angela, *The Other Side of the Coin: The Queen, the Dresser and the Wardrobe*, HarperCollins, 2022

King-Hall, Magdalen, *The Story of the Nursery*, Routledge & Kegan Paul, 1958

Kiste, John Van Der, *George V's Children*, Alan Sutton, 1991

Kiste, John Van Der, *Queen Victoria's Children*, History Press, 2009

Kiste, John Van Der, *William and Mary: Heroes of the Glorious Revolution*, History Press, 2008

Kroll, Maria, *Sophie, Electress of Hanover: A Personal Portrait*, Gollancz, 1973

Lacey, Robert, *Majesty: Elizabeth II and the House of Windsor*, Hutchinson, 1977

Lane, Peter, *Prince Philip*, Robert Hale, 1980

Lascelles, Alan, *King's Counsellor: Abdication and War: The Diaries of Sir Alan 'Tommy Lascelles*, ed. Duff Hart-Davis, Weidenfeld & Nicolson, 2020

Latham, Jean, *Happy Families: Growing Up in the Eighteenth and Nineteenth Centuries*, Adam & Charles Black, 1974

Law, Ernest, *Kensington Palace: Birthplace of Queen Victoria*, G. Bell & Sons, 1909

Leslie, Anita, *Edwardians in Love*, Arrow Books, 1974

Levi, Anthony, *Louis XIV*, Constable, 2004

Liversidge, Douglas, *Prince Charles: Monarch in the Making*, Panther, 1979

Loftie, William John, *Kensington Palace and Gardens*, Farmer & Sons, 1900

Longford, Elizabeth, *The Royal House of Windsor*, Weidenfeld & Nicolson, 1974

Longford, Elizabeth, *Victoria R. I.*, Weidenfeld & Nicolson, 1964

Longford, Paul, *Eighteenth-Century Britain*, Oxford University Press, 1984

Lowe, Valentine, *Courtiers: The Hidden Power Behind the Crown*, Headline, 2022

Lownie, Andrew, *The Mountbattens: Their Lives and Loves*, Blink Publishing, 2020

Lynd, Sylvia, *English Children*, William Collins, 1942

Lyttelton, Lady Sarah, *Correspondence 1787–1870*, ed. Hon. Mrs Hugh Wyndham, John Murray, 1912

Machiavelli, Niccolò, *The Prince*, Oxford World's Classics, 2008

Mackenzie, Compton, *The Windsor Tapestry*, Rich and Cowan, 1938

Magnus, Philip, *King Edward the Seventh*, John Murray, 1964

Malcolm, James Peller, *Anecdotes of the Manners and Customs of London During the Eighteenth Century*, Longman, 1810

Marie-Louise, Princess, *My Memories of Six Reigns*, Evans Brothers, 1956

Marot, Christopher, *Victoria's Other Self*, unpublished PhD

Martin, Brian P., *The Great Shoots*, Quiller, 2018

Melville, Lewis, *Lady Suffolk and Her Circle*, Hutchinson, 1924

Mitford, Nancy, 'U and Non-U', *Encounter* magazine, 1955

Mortimer, Ian, *The Time Traveller's Guide to the Restoration*, Vintage, 2018

Morton, Andrew, *17 Carnations: The Windsors, the Nazis and the Cover-Up*, Michael O'Mara, 2015

Morton, Andrew, *Diana: Her True Story*, Michael O'Mara, 1992

Morton, Andrew, *Inside Kensington Palace*, Michael O'Mara, 1987

Mosley, Nicholas, *Beyond the Pale*, Secker, 1983

Muir, Richard, *Portraits of the Past*, Michael Joseph, 1989

Murphy, N. T. P., *One Man's London*, Hutchinson, 1989

Newsome, David, *The Victorian World Picture*, John Murray, 1997

Nicolson, Harold, *George V: His Life and Reign*, Constable, 1952

Nicolson, Nigel, *Long Life*, Weidenfeld & Nicolson, 1997

Nicolson, Nigel, *Portrait of a Marriage*, Weidenfeld & Nicolson, 2014

Ogilvy, Mabell, *Thatched with Gold: The Memoirs of Mabell, Countess of Airlie*, ed. Jennifer Ellis, Cedric Chivers, 1972

Orme, Nicholas, *Medieval Children*, Yale University Press, 2001

Pain, N., *George III at Home*, Eyre Methuen, 1975

Pakula, Anna, *An Uncommon Woman: The Life of Princess Vicky*, Weidenfeld & Nicolson, 2006

Pasternak, Anna, *Untitled: The Real Wallis Simpson*, William Collins, 2019

Pepys, Samuel, *The Diary*, ed. Robert Latham and William Matthews, Bell & Hyman, 1985

Picard, Lisa, *Everyday Life in the 1660s*, Weidenfeld & Nicolson, 2004

Picard, Lisa, *Victorian London: The Life of a City 1840–1870*, Weidenfeld & Nicolson, 2006

Pinchbeck, Ivy, and Hewitt, Margaret, *Children in English Society*, Routledge & Kegan Paul, 1969

Plantagenet, Arthur, *The Lisle Letters*, ed. Muriel St Clare Byrne, University of Chicago Press, 1981

Plowden, Alison, *The Young Elizabeth*, Macmillan, 1971

Plowden, Alison, *The Young Victoria*, Macmillan, 1981

Pope-Hennessy, James, *Queen Mary*, Allen & Unwin, 1954

Pope-Hennessy, James, and Hugo Vickers, *The Quest for Queen Mary*, Hodder, 2019

Prescott, H. F. M., *Mary Tudor*, Eyre & Spottiswoode, 1940

Pyne, William Henry, *The History of the Royal Residences*, London, 1819

Quinn, Tom, *Backstairs Billy: The Life of William Tallon, the Queen Mother's Most Devoted Servant*, Biteback Publishing, 2015

Quinn, Tom, *BB Remembered: The Life and Times of Denys Watkins-Pitchford*, Quiller, 2006

Quinn, Tom, *The Butler's Tale*, Coronet, 2012

Quinn, Tom, *The Maid's Tale*, Coronet 2011

Quinn, Tom, *Mrs Keppel: Mistress to the King*, Biteback Publishing, 2016

Rhodes, Hugh, *The Book of Nurture*, Thomass Cast, London, 1560

Rhodes, Margaret, *A Final Curtsey*, Birlinn, 2012

Ridley, Jane, *Bertie: A life of Edward VII*, Chatto, 2012

Ring, Anne, *The Story of Princess Elizabeth*, John Murray, 1930

Robertson-Scott, J. W., *The Story of the Pall Mall Gazette*, Oxford University Press, 1950

Rochester, John Wilmot, Earl of, *Complete Poems*, ed. David Vieth, Yale University Press, 1968

Rochester, John Wilmot, Earl of, *The Rochester-Savile Letters 1671–1680*, ed. John Wilson, Ohio State University Press, 1941

Roe, F. G., *The Georgian Child*, Phoenix House, 1961

Rose, Kenneth, *King George V*, Weidenfeld & Nicolson, 1983

Rousseau, Jean-Jacques, *Emile: On Education*, Penguin, 1991Rubin, Miri, *The Hollow Crown*, Penguin, 2005

Russell, Bertrand, *Autobiography, 1872–1914*, Allen & Unwin, 1967

St Aubyn, Giles, *Edward VII: Prince and King*, Harper Collins, 1979

Saussure, César, *A Foreign View of England in 1725–1729*, trs M. van Muyden, John Murray, 1902

Scobie, Omid and Carolyn Durand, *Finding Freedom: Harry and Meghan and the making of a modern royal family*, HQ, 2021

Sebba, Anne, *That Woman: The Life of Wallis Simpson, Duchess of Windsor*, Phoenix, 2012

Seward, Ingrid, *Diana*, Weidenfeld & Nicolson, 1988

Seward, Ingrid, *Royal Children of the Twentieth Century*, Harper Collins, 1993

Seward, Ingrid, *Sarah, HRH The Duchess of York*, Harper Collins, 1991

Shaw, Karl, *Eccentrics and Oddballs*, Robinson, 2000

Sim, Alison, *Masters and Servants in Tudor England*, Sutton, 2006

Simms, R. S., *Kensington Palace*, HMSO, 1936

Sinclair, David, *Queen and Country: The Life of Queen Elizabeth the Queen Mother*, Dent, 1979

Somerset, Anne, *Ladies in Waiting*, Weidenfeld & Nicolson, 1984

Somerset, Anne, *Queen Anne: The Politics of Passion*, Harper, 2012

Sorbière, Samuel de, *A Voyage to England*, London, 1709

Spinks, Stephen, *Edward the Man*, Amberley, 2019

Spufford, Peter, *Power and Profit: The Merchant in Medieval Europe*, Thames & Hudson, 2002

Stanley, Lady Augusta, *Letters 1849–63*, ed. Hector Bolitho, Gerald Howe, 1927

Stockmar, Baron Christian Friedrich, *Memoirs*, ed. Baron E. Stockmar, trs. G. A. Muller, Longmans, 1872

Strachey, Lytton, *Eminent Victorians*, Chatto, 1918

Strachey, Lytton, *Queen Victoria*, Chatto, 1921

Stuart, Dorothy Margaret, *The Daughters of George II*, Macmillan, 1939

Sundon, Viscountess, *Memoirs*, 2 vols, Henry Colburn, 1847

Synge, V. M., *Royal Guides*, Girl Guides Association, 1948

Thackeray, William Makepeace, *The Four Georges and the English Humourists*, Alan Sutton, 1995

Thomas, Albert, *Wait and See*, Michael Joseph, 1944

Thomas, Keith, *The Ends of Life*, Oxford University Press, 2009

Thompson, E. P., *The Making of the English Working Class*, Penguin, 2013

Thoms, William, et al., *Anecdotes and Traditions Illustrative of Early English History*, Camden Society, 1839

Thornbury, Walter, *Old and New London*, Cassell, 1878

Thorold, Peter, *The London Rich*, Viking, 1999

Thurley, Simon, *The Royal Palaces of Tudor England*, Paul Mellon Centre for Studies in British Art, 1993

Tinniswood, Adrian, *Behind the Throne: A Domestic History of the Royal Household*, Vintage, 2018

Tinniswood, Adrian, *His Invention So Fertile: A Life of Sir Christopher Wren*, Cape, 2001

Trethewey, Rachel, *Before Wallis: Edward VIII's Other Women*, History Press, 2020

Trevelyan, George Macaulay, *The England of Queen Anne*, Longmans, 1932

Trevisano, Andrea, *A Relation, or Rather True Account of the Island of England*, trs. Charlotte Sneyd, London, 1847

Troost, Wout, *William III, The Stadholder King: A Political Biography*, Routledge, 2005

Tschumi, Gabriel, *Royal Chef: Recollections of Life in Royal Households*, William Kimber, 1954

Vansittart, Peter, *London: A Literary Companion*, John Murray, 1992

Vergil, Polydore, *Anglica Historia*, trs. and ed. Denys Hays, Office of the Royal Historical Society, 1950

Vickers, Hugo, *Elizabeth the Queen*, Arrow Books, 2006

Vickery, Amanda, *Behind Closed Doors: At Home in Georgian England*, Yale University Press, 2009

Vickery, Amanda, *The Gentleman's Daughter: Women's Lives in Georgian England*, Yale University Press, 1998

Victoria, Queen, *Leaves from the Journal of our Life in the Highlands from 1841 to 1868*, Smith Elder, 1868

Victoria, Queen, *Letters*, John Murray, 1907

Victoria, Queen, *More Leaves from a Journal of Our Life in the Highlands*, Smith Elder, 1884

Vincent, James E., *HRH The Duke of Clarence and Avondale*, John Murray, 1893

Wadlow, Flo, *Over a Hot Stove: A Kitchen Maid's Story*, Mousehold Press, 2007

Wakeford, Geoffrey, *The Princesses Royal*, Hale, 1973

Walpole, Horace, *Reminiscences*, Clarendon Press, 1924

Warner, Katherine, *Edward II*, Amberley, 2014

Warner, Marina, *Queen Victoria's Sketchbook*, Macmillan, 1979

Warwick, Frances, Countess of, *Life's Ebb and Flow*, Hutchinson, 1929

Weinreb, Ben and Christopher Hibbert, *The London Encyclopaedia*, Macmillan, 2010

Weintraub, Stanley, *Uncrowned King: The Life of Prince Albert*, John Murray, 1997

Weintraub, Stanley, *Victoria: Biography of a Queen*, Harper, 1987

Weir, Alison, *Elizabeth the Queen*, Vintage, 2009

Weldon, Sir Anthony, *A Brief History of the Kings of England*, J. Williams, 1766

Weldon, Sir Anthony, *The Court and Character of Kings James*, Smeeton's Historical and Biographical Tracts, 1817

Wheeler-Bennett, Sir John, *The Life and Reign of George VI*, Macmillan, 1958

Wheen, Francis, *Tom Driberg: His Life and Indiscretions*, Fourth Estate, 2001

Williams-Wynne, Frances, *Diaries of a Lady of Quality, from 1797 to 1844*, ed. A. Hayward, Longmans, 1864

Wilson, A. N., *After the Victorians*, Picador, 2006

Wilson, A. N., *Victoria: A Life*, Atlantic, 2014

Windsor, Duke of, *A Family Album*, Cassell, 1960

Windsor, Duke of, *A King's Story: The memoirs of HRH the Duke of Windsor*, Cassell, 1960

Wormald, Patrick, *The Making of English Law*, Blackwells, 1999

Wormald, Patrick, *The Uses of Literacy in Anglo-Saxon England and Its Neighbours*, Cambridge University Press, 1977

Worsley, Lucy, *Courtiers: The Secret History of Kensington Palace*, Faber, 2010

York, Rosemary, *Charles in His Own Words*, W. H. Allen, 1981

Zall, P. M. (ed.), *A Nest of Ninnies and Other English Jestbooks of the Seventeenth Century*, University of Nebraska Press, 1970

Acknowledgements

Thanks to the staff at the British Library, who managed to find even the most obscure books and papers for me despite their computer system being out of action for more than two years following a major hack.

Thanks also to my personal team of eagle-eyed historians and royal watchers – Charlotte, Alex, James, Katy, Joe and Mattie. And last but by no means least – a huge thank-you to Olivia and James at Biteback for commissioning me to write *Yes Ma'am* and my other royal books in the first place.

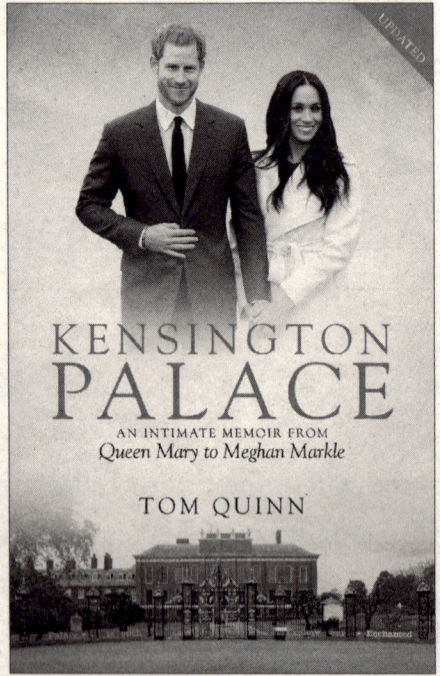